PLANTING
A GARDEN

Growing the Church
Beyond Traditional Models

LINDA S. MCCOY

Abingdon Press
Nashville

PLANTING A GARDEN
GROWING THE CHURCH BEYOND TRADITIONAL MODELS

Library of Congress Cataloging-in-Publication Data

McCoy, Linda Schiphorst, 1945-
   Planting a garden : growing the church beyond traditional models / Linda S. McCoy.
      p. cm.
   ISBN 0-687-34314-3 (binding: pbk. : alk. paper)
   1. Church growth.   2. Garden (Church : Indianapolis, Ind.)   I. Title.

BV652.25.M219 2005
253'.7—dc22

                                                                        2004024658

05 06 07 08 09 10 11 12 13 14—10 9 8 7 6 5 4 3 2 1

MANUFACTURED IN THE UNITED STATES OF AMERICA

To my husband, Mike,
who has been a wonderful partner in life
and in ministry for many years.
Thank you for your loving support and encouragement.

To all those who work so faithfully every day to make The
Garden what it is.
Without your love and commitment,
we would never have been able to take this journey.

Finally, to the memory of Mary Benedict,
Garden publications founder and editor,
whose tireless commitment
to The Garden moved us light years forward.

CONTENTS

FOREWORD

D r. Linda McCoy is one of the most creative, committed, and competent pastors I know. Dr. McCoy began her professional career as a high school French teacher, became an active lay member of St. Luke's United Methodist Church, and then felt God's call to the ordained ministry. This means that Linda is a second-career pastor and consequently has a deep feeling and understanding of how laypersons in the congregation feel and respond to pastoral leadership.

Linda became a part-time staff member of St. Luke's in 1982, leading a program called "The Shepherding Ministry," which organized all of the congregation's members into geographical ministry groups with a shepherding leader caring for the pastoral and personal needs of each family in his or her group. While working part time at the church, Linda completed her Master of Divinity degree at Christian Theological Seminary, graduating at the top of her class in 1985.

Linda continued her education by completing her Doctor of Ministry degree in 1995 from United Theological Seminary in Dayton, Ohio, with her dissertation focusing on the positive contributions of women in ministry.

However, I believe that Linda really hit her stride as a creative and innovative leader when she felt God's call to begin a new ministry at St. Luke's. In 1994, Linda came to see me and told me that she had felt a divine calling to begin something "new" in ministry though she was not completely sure what it would look like. I told her that when someone has a divine calling, I want to be on God's side and supportive of that call.

Linda and her good friend Suzanne Stark began to travel around the country, visiting growing churches that had contemporary or nontraditional services. They discovered that many of the churches that had these services were theologically conservative though they were progressive in their use of movie clips, bands, drama, and other nontraditional forms of worship. They began to envision a nontraditional service that was progressive in both the theology and the method and style of the worship experience.

After almost a year of researching and enrolling a team of supporters for this new ministry, Linda and Suzanne launched The Garden, a nontraditional satellite worship experience at Beef and Boards Dinner Theatre about four miles west of St. Luke's campus.

Linda's vision, commitment, competence, and compassion for people have reaped huge results in terms of the numbers of people who have felt the unconditional love of God through The Garden ministries. Today The Garden has three services at Beef and Boards, with about five hundred people in average attendance, and has started another nontraditional satellite service at the Oak Hill Mansion, a banquet and catering mansion located about eight miles east of St. Luke's that has almost two hundred in average attendance each Sunday.

We believe that churches will grow in outreach and attendance when they begin to provide more alternative types of worship experiences. The worship attendance growth at St. Luke's was steady but modest when we just had three traditional worship services. However, when we started multiple types and times for worship, the average annual attendance increased exponentially. In 1992, the average worship attendance at St. Luke's was about eighteen hundred each Sunday; but in 2004, the average attendance in our ten weekly services is about thirty-three hundred.

We believe that any creative and visionary congregation can begin to reach more people with the good news of God's unconditional love by creating indigenous worship services that reach new groups of people by providing the types and style of worship experiences that meet their needs and touch their hearts.

In this book, Dr. McCoy tells the story of The Garden and models for others how they, too, might begin nontraditional worship services either at their current location or at satellite locations. My prayer is that Linda's story will inspire many church leaders to think creatively and "outside the box" so others will come to experience God's unconditional love in their own lives.

Kent Millard
Lead Pastor
St. Luke's United Methodist Church

A WORD OF WELCOME TO THE GARDEN

Welcome to the story of what we believe to be a wonderful journey of faith. It is the story of The Garden in Indianapolis, Indiana. For those of you who are considering moving down a new path of what it means to be church, I welcome you aboard. This book will offer some helpful ideas and some specific steps that you can implement on your adventure.

Even those who are not currently exploring a different way to be church will find something to think about and chew on in these pages. You may not agree with everything I'm writing, and perhaps not with any of it, and that's OK. I do hope this book will cause you to become engaged in the conversation of the mission of the church in the future, and how we can faithfully live out God's call on our lives. Enjoy the journey, and let the story begin.

Linda S. McCoy

"IN THE BEGINNING . . ."

God planted the seeds of what was to become The Garden, A *Blossom of St. Luke's United Methodist Church*, in November 1994. It was a time of great angst and inner turmoil for me. After twenty-six idyllic years as senior pastor of St. Luke's, Dr. E. Carver McGriff retired. We had enjoyed many years as a clergy staff of six under his leadership, and St. Luke's had thrived. All of us were wondering what our future held after this change.

A new senior pastor, Dr. Kent Millard, arrived at St. Luke's in October 1993, and almost immediately, the inevitable changes that come with new leadership began to occur. Several of my colleagues decided it was time for them to move on to other churches, and they began that process with our District Superintendent. I, too, was willing to open myself to appointment in another setting, if that were the will of the Bishop and Cabinet. Maybe it was time to move on; maybe it was even time for me to consider leaving pastoral ministry and begin to pursue another profession or undertaking. I was uncertain what the future held, but I knew when I was asked to consider becoming the chaplain at one of our denomination's retirement homes, I was clear on one thing—that was definitely not for me! And so the turmoil continued.

In 1993, another colleague and I were invited to begin studies for a Doctor of Ministry degree from United Theological Seminary, and we had a unique opportunity in the course of those studies. We were an all–United Methodist clergy group, and our mentors were Michael Slaughter and Tom Tumblin, who were instrumental to the growth of

Ginghamsburg United Methodist Church in Tipp City, Ohio. The focus during our years there was on the meta model of ministry, a small group model of ministry begun in the churches of Korea. We were fortunate enough to be able to travel to Korea to observe that small group model in action.

In the course of my studies and under the tenure of a new senior pastor, I once again engaged in dialogue with my District Superintendent, a man new to the job. I told him that I was willing to be considered for another appointment and that I thought I had some interest in a "new church start." There was a floundering new church start in our district, and there were some preliminary conversations about my moving to that location; but in mid-November 1994, both the District Superintendent and I mutually agreed that it was not the right thing.

The day after that conversation, I was on a plane flying to Denver to conduct some interviews in the Denver Area for my doctoral project. After much deliberation, I had chosen to focus my attention on women in ministry and was in the process of creating a video that highlighted the experiences of clergywomen in The United Methodist Church. At that time, Mary Ann Swenson was bishop of the Rocky Mountain conference, and there were several women in high-profile positions there. A friend, the Reverend Ed Paup, now a bishop in the Seattle Area, arranged for me to conduct several interviews with some of those women.

The anxiety and inner conflict that resulted from the one-day-old discussion with my District Superintendent about the church start "non-appointment" was very much on my mind as I boarded the plane to head west. What would happen now? Was there any hope that I would continue in ministry, or was God calling me in a new direction?

One of the books I was reading on the plane as preparation for my doctoral work was a book by business guru Tom Peters. It was entitled *The Tom Peters Seminar: Crazy Times Call for Crazy Organizations* (New York: Vintage Books, 1994). In that book, Peters tells a story about a Japanese gentleman who went to his boss and asked, "What do you want me to do? What do you want me to make?" His boss answered simply, "Make something great!" And the worker invented Nintendo.

After reading that story, I fell asleep, and I had a dream. I can't tell you the specifics of the dream; I only know that when I awoke, all the struggle and turmoil from the past year had evaporated, and I was filled with a sense of peace and calm that has never left me. Although I couldn't know then the form it would ultimately take, I knew for certain that I was supposed to be doing something far different from anything I had ever done before in ministry. I knew one thing for sure: this was definitely a revelation from God!

When I returned to Indianapolis after a few days in Denver, I told Kent Millard what had happened on that plane. His words to me were: "If this is from God, I want to be on God's side!" With those words of endorsement and encouragement, we were off and running!

Fortunately, we were off and running in a church that has a long history of encouraging people to find their passion and follow it. Never has an idea had to go through the red tape of committee after committee study, discussion, and approval. Given the size and vitality of St. Luke's, it's possible to find folks who are positive and enthusiastic about an opportunity for mission, and a spirit of hope pervades every venture there. That was certainly true when it came to the seeding of this new ministry.

The pages that follow tell the story of what happened in the weeks and months and years ahead; and they share some of our learnings, as well as some of the experiences we have had on this journey— experiences that assure us that God is indeed doing "a new thing" in the world today. We don't profess to have all the answers, nor do we believe this is the only way to be the church today. We do believe that we have gained some insights and discovered some hints about how to reach out to those who have never experienced the unconditional love of God. Perhaps some of the ideas will take root in your hearts and minds and spirits, and you, too, will discover the "new thing" that God has in store for you and your congregation.

CHAPTER 1

THE GARDEN TODAY

The Garden, *A Blossom of St. Luke's United Methodist Church*, in Indianapolis, Indiana, is an off-site satellite congregation that holds three services each Sunday in a dinner theater and one identical service every Sunday morning in a banquet facility. Planning for The Garden, although it wasn't yet called that, began in December 1994. The early seeds that were planted were nuggets of conversations about what it would be like to have a church that looked very different from the traditional services that so many found uplifting at St. Luke's. Several of the leaders of the congregation encouraged us to proceed, and a core from St. Luke's agreed to give us a year of their time and energy to help launch the new ministry. Teams began to form, and the ministry began to take shape. The first worship service was held on September 10, 1995, after nine months of intense dreaming, envisioning, praying, hoping, and planning.

From its meager beginnings, with about two hundred in worship on that first Sunday, to today, The Garden has shown rather consistent growth. Currently, worship attendance hovers between six hundred and seven hundred on any given Sunday. After increasing the number of worship services from one to two to three, the theater was at maximum capacity. In January 2003, The Garden expanded to a second site, and that has created a new set of challenges, which you will read about later.

But back to the beginning: The group that gathered to create this new way of being church simply talked about what kind of service we would like to attend. Those early conversations were influential in determining our core values and how those values influenced everything we did on Sundays, as well as throughout the week. While the planning process will be discussed in greater detail later on, suffice it to say that we did a lot of reading, visiting, researching, and sorting through what we wanted this ministry to become.

One thing became clear to us: we wanted to reach those who had not responded to the traditional appeals of the church. We wanted to connect with those who had found themselves "turned out" or "turned off" by their previous church experience. We wanted to create a worship experience in which there was no delineation between insiders and outsiders, between members and nonmembers. We wanted people to walk in our doors and feel welcomed and accepted, and we didn't want to make it necessary for them to know the language of the church or any of its ways that can seem so mysterious and incomprehensible to "outsiders."

Our byword has become: "No prior experience required." Those who arrive at The Garden are not expected to know the words to the Lord's Prayer, the Gloria Patria, or the Doxology. They do not need to know the "in" language or traditions of conventional church. They do not, unlike Mr. Bean in the classic *Mr. Bean Goes to Church*, have to guess when to stand and when to sit, nor do they have to stumble through strange words sung to unfamiliar tunes. In other words, we have attempted to create services that reduce and lower any of the church barriers that keep people from a relationship with God. Even though the current United Methodist slogan, "Open hearts, open minds, open doors," did not yet exist, The Garden created an experience that exemplified those words.

When people enter either of our sites, Beef and Boards Dinner Theater or The Mansion at Oak Hill, on Sunday mornings, a very different experience awaits them. Newcomers don't have to wander around the facility, wondering where they're to go and what they're to do. They are greeted in the parking lot, and there they get a first glimpse of what the morning will be like. Greeters inside Beef and Boards and Oak Hill hand them a program, which isn't really an order of worship, but rather, a summary of the morning's theme, along with a few pertinent announcements. An information table in the lobby offers informative brochures, and flyers of special events are found on the table.

There's no need to run through the drive-through at McDonald's before going to church at The Garden. Children often refer to it as "the donut church" or "the bagel church." That's because our guests are invited to get a cup of coffee or some juice, grab a bagel or a muffin or a donut, and munch away while the service is in progress. If the coffee cup is empty, Gardeners feel free to walk over and refill the cup. Families, singles, couples, and large and small gatherings of friends sit around tables, catching up with one another before the services, holding hands during prayer time, hugging one another during a special song. Gathering at tables and enjoying some food for the body opens the door for receiving food for the spirit. In fact, The Garden's jingle, which opens almost every service, begins with the words: "In The Garden, there's hope, and food for the soul.... Helpful words to make your life whole." Our logo includes the phrases: "Food for the spirit; wisdom for the soul." The words of both the opening and the logo capture the essence of what we hope Gardeners experience each and every Sunday morning.

Once the service begins, newcomers are in for a surprise. There are no hymns to sing or creeds to recite. There are no verses on a screen with the words to praise choruses on them. Instead a very talented band may rock the place with a U2 song, or maybe it's the twangy sounds of Shania Twain. The music that many of us hear on our favorite light rock or country stations may be just the music that carries the theme of the day. One thing is for sure, after hearing the words to a song at The Garden, their meaning is forever changed in our hearts and minds.

Once upon a time, the oral tradition ruled. Stories were passed from generation to generation by word of mouth, but that is not the case today. We understand that people learn and receive the message in a variety of ways. That's why we try to create a multisensory experience for our attendees, knowing that some will "get it" from the spoken words, but others will be touched by a song, and others will connect with the message through a movie clip—movies being the art form of our day and of younger generations. A comedy sketch or a humorous way of presenting the Bible passage (which is almost always a modern language version) can introduce and reinforce the morning's theme in a way that a sermon could never begin to do. Because of what we have learned about how people receive and integrate the message of hope and love and joy and peace, we try to offer a blending of ingredients that flow together into an integrated whole.

The Garden has surprised us with the diversity of those who attend. It is a diverse worshiping community, which is made up of people who are Caucasian, African American, Filipino, Chinese, Native American, Jamaican, and Zimbabwean. Until recently, twenty or more residents of St. Vincent Hospital Assisted Living Program (consisting of people who are in recovery programs for alcohol and substance abuse) came to The Garden by a city bus each week. Although that program has closed, many of the graduates of the program continue to be stalwarts at our services, and moves are afoot to reach out in different ways to those in recovery.

The Garden is also diverse in terms of age, economics, education, sexual orientation, and work life. When it comes to geographic distance, Gardeners come to us from as close as one mile and as far as sixty miles away. There are families with children who worship with us regularly, and we are nearly equally divided between those who are married and those who are single. Likewise, those who are single represent a cross section of never married, divorced, and widowed, as well as a number who are in committed relationships (both heterosexual and homosexual).

Those who attend The Garden represent a vast range of prior church experience. Some have never had any exposure to "church" and never imagined that anything spiritual would ever be relevant to their lives. A recent survey indicated that approximately two-thirds of Gardeners fall into that category. Others have had past experience with a church, but have been either turned off or turned out by it. They have been disappointed and disillusioned. Still others are members of a church but, for whatever reason, have become inactive and have rediscovered the connection through The Garden. And there are still others who have always been involved with the traditional church but find their experience at The Garden to be one that revives their spirits.

One of the reasons I believe The Garden has become the spiritual home for such a diverse group of people is that it is not housed in a church building. For many, the imposing structure of many of our churches can seem like foreign territory; it can be a foreboding, intimidating place for many to enter. For those unfamiliar with the church, there are no warm, comforting memories to make a church building a safe place.

Being housed in a secular facility has been a real advantage for us. Going into a dinner theater to see a Broadway production is a fun thing, and the theater offers a welcoming presence. Walking into a facility that one has visited at a party or reception lowers the level of discomfort. Most people are definitely more at ease going into a movie theater, for example, than going into a hospital. The same logic holds true for a building designed for business purposes, rather than the "holiest of holies" designed for the worship of God.

Lest you think that The Garden is solely a Sunday morning alternative worship experience, allow me to clarify. The main focus of our week, as for any church, is what happens on Sunday morning. We spend a great deal of time and energy preparing for it, but Sunday worship is only one of the many things that happens at The Garden.

We have eighteen different teams that carry on the functions of this ministry. Our Garden Leadership Team is the "dream team." This team tries to stay away from the nuts and bolts of the day-to-day ministry by just keeping informed on what's going on in general. Their main role is that of encouragement and visioning. They focus on the big picture.

We have teams that are directly connected with worship design, as in, for example, our two bands/music teams, Worship Design Team, Video Team, Tech Team, and Creative Team. Our Hospitality Teams are vital in making each Sunday morning a pleasant and memorable experience for those who attend. Other teams such as the Communication Team and Marketing Team concentrate on getting the word out to Gardeners and to the community beyond our doors. Our Comfort and Care Team is composed of laypersons who make contacts in the event of hospitalization or death, and we have several trained Stephen Ministers who offer specialized one-on-one assistance. (Stephen Ministries is a national program of thorough, systematic training for laypersons in pastoral care.) Our Development Team oversees the financial matters of The Garden. The Outreach Team and the Charitable Contributions Team serve to keep us outwardly focused. In addition, there are numerous other teams that form around a special project and work for a designated span of time before disbanding. These have become our small groups.

Although we do not use the small group method that is so popular in many churches, there are opportunities for making connections with other Gardeners through some study opportunities. Currently there are three different book study options from which Gardeners can choose, and a group of singles gathers for brunch every other Sunday. A Garden youth group was formed last year. Each of those groups has arisen from a need for Gardeners to connect with one another. In addition to these opportunities, everything that's a part of the many educational and spiritual offerings at St. Luke's is always open to the community at large, and certainly to any and all Garden folks.

It's probably helpful to understand that The Garden is really a church within the larger church of St. Luke's, and our congregation is larger than the majority of congregations in our geographical area. Although we are very much a part of St. Luke's and benefit from its stellar reputation in the community and its many excellent programs, we also operate independently.

From the very beginning, the fundamental connecting point, other than my twenty-two years of tenure on the staff of St. Luke's, is the relationship that Kent Millard, senior pastor of St. Luke's, and I have forged. Without a solid relationship built on the trust and respect we have for each other, this mutually beneficial ministry could not thrive the way it has over the last eight-plus years. It is important for me to acknowledge the incredible encouragement and support I have received from Kent and from the St. Luke's congregation both before and since The Garden began.

Even though we have close connections with the "big church" (St. Luke's), The Garden still operates in a fairly independent manner. We will discuss finances in a later chapter, but a brief statement about the financial arrangements might be helpful here. St. Luke's pays my compensation package and provides office space for The Garden. St. Luke's also pays for our part-time second-site anchors, one who is an ordained Disciples pastor, and one who is a full-time seminary student. The Garden pays for the remainder of its staff, which includes two full-time administrative team members, our creative director, three keyboardists, two sound and light technicians, and an expert video producer. In addition, we pay for all the other resources needed to conduct a full-fledged ministry. In 2004, that budget figure will approach $500,000. With the help of generous contributors, along with grants from our annual conference, we are able to have zero effect on the budgeting of St. Luke's, with the exception of the pastoral personnel.

One of the independent decisions The Garden made several years ago was to keep our attention focused outwardly. It is sometimes easy to become navel-gazers and care only for ourselves, but The Garden is an outreach ministry, and we want to reach out in whatever way we can to make our community and world a better place. One way in which we do that is with our charitable organization contribution. Each month The Garden selects a different local organization and gives 10 percent of our Sunday offerings to that group. In addition, we prepare a 3- to 4-minute video of the group's work, and donate that video to the group to help them raise both funds and awareness. This is a professionally produced video whose value is in the $5,000 to $10,000 range.

The mention of Sunday offerings causes me to note another difference that a visitor will find at The Garden, and that is the absence of an offering or collection plate during the service. Knowing that one of the main complaints nonchurch people have against the church is "all they ever do is ask for money," we made a conscious decision to buck that trend. We do not collect an offering during the service. Instead, we have watering cans at the door, and there are slides that appear on screen prior to the service inviting financial support for The Garden. There are also envelopes on the table for attendees to use if they so desire.

There are several key factors that have been important to The Garden and its ministry. The integrated Sunday service is one of them. Having all the music, videos, prayers, drama and comedy sketches, and message tie to a central theme is powerful in carrying the message of God's unconditional love. No one should leave The Garden after any given service and wonder what it was about that day. We strive to integrate everything as well as we can and to share our hope and joy in the best way that we can. It is interesting to note that parents report that their children, too, remember and discuss the theme in the car on the way home, and even during the ensuing week.

Creating a welcoming and nonthreatening atmosphere is another important facet of The Garden. Newcomers are welcomed and assisted in whatever way is needed, but they are not smothered. Most tell us that they appreciate not being singled out in the service as a new person, and they also appreciate the opportunity to tell us whether or not they desire a follow-up contact. We do not take bread or cookies to their door, but ask on an information card, which visitors can voluntarily fill out, "May we contact you?" If no is checked, we do not make the contact.

Having so many gifted unpaid staff members has been a godsend! The preparation we do each week is labor-intensive, and volunteers give hundreds of hours each week to make sure everything happens as it is supposed to happen. They give of themselves because they believe in The Garden, and they have felt the touch of God through using their talents to share God's love and grace with others. Working together in teams means sharing one another's joys and burdens. Because of the bonds that have been created, we have laughed together and cried together, held hands with one another, and held on for dear life! What a blessing it has been for me to know and be able to work with such loving, dedicated, faith-filled people!

We describe our ministry with these words: "The Garden is a celebration of life, a journey into faith, and the soulful embrace of all." By that, we mean that life is good and is to be celebrated. We laugh and share the joy of living each day as it comes to us. We believe that faith is a journey, not a destination. Therefore, we are growing and evolving in our relationship with God, and it's OK to question and wonder and wander and doubt. That's part of the journey. By the phrase "the soulful embrace of all," we mean that everyone is welcome. It does not matter where we have been, or what we have done, everyone is welcome. Spirit to spirit, soul to soul, we are brothers and sisters together.

The mission of The Garden is as follows: "The Garden seeks to engage all in the quest to know and share the unconditional love of God." We want to engage Gardeners on a deeper level and help each one of us get on the journey to draw closer to God and to one another. Our faith doesn't stop with our knowing God's love on a personal level; it is something we must share. We seek ways to help people know that love, and to share it in ways that make our world a more loving, more compassionate place in which to live.

We have tried to be faithful to the Great Commission which, for us, is summarized best in one verse from Today's English Version of the Bible: "Go, then, to all peoples everywhere and make them my disciples" (Matthew 28:19).

CHAPTER 2

ENVISIONING THE GARDEN

But [God] says,
"Do not cling to events of the past
or dwell on what happened long ago.
Watch for the new thing I am going to do.
It is happening already—you can see it now!"
Isaiah 43:18-19

"A God-Thing"

God is always creating, bringing new things, new ideas, new concepts into being. Although there are those who believe that God quit interacting with humanity at the dawn of creation, the world around us points to a very different reality. God is indeed very much among us, connecting with us, and offering new revelations. It is for us to be open to see and receive that which God is trying to reveal.

For a new ministry to be viable, it must be a "God-thing," a direction in which God is leading us. The tendency among many congregations is to do "contemporary" worship because everyone is doing it, and it seems to be succeeding. As I look around the church, I see many efforts to duplicate what other congregations such as Willow Creek or Saddleback are doing. These attempts may have modest success; but ultimately, if there is not a strong sense of vision, passion, and call to a different style of ministry, it will not thrive or survive.

All too often, I see churches trying to copy what someone else is doing and, in the process, failing to be true to who they are and where God is calling them to minister. It is my opinion that we don't do something for numerical growth, nor because it's the thing to do, but rather because it is clear to the leaders and congregations that this direction is of God.

How do we know that God is revealing something new for us? I shared in the introduction how God revealed the seeds for The Garden to me through a dream, and I do believe that as we find in the Bible with Jacob and others, a dream is one of the ways in which God can work. However, I believe that God works in and through some very ordinary ways to connect with us, too. Maybe it's just a word or a thought that comes to us in the midst of our work day. Perhaps it's a persistent idea that won't evaporate, or it's the awareness of a pressing need that we could meet.

For us at The Garden, once the impetus from the dream moved us toward action, things began to converge. It wasn't so much a part of a plan, although there was one. Rather it was that "coincidences" began to happen; people began to emerge; facilities became available. I have a friend who refers to these kinds of happenings as "God-cidences," and I think he's right. It's a matter of being aware of them and ready to seize the opportunities that present themselves to us. If what we are undertaking is a God-thing, doors will open.

Once we have opened our eyes to see what God has in mind for our ministry, how do we find the courage to follow? Walt Kallestad, senior pastor of Community Church of Joy in Glendale, Arizona, says, "The essence of faith is risk." We've found that to be true. When The Garden began to take shape, we didn't have a clear idea of exactly what it would look like. We didn't know if it would become a separate "new church start," or if it would remain a satellite of a thriving suburban congregation. We didn't know if anyone would attend on the first Sunday, or, if they did, if they would return in subsequent weeks. We were trying something far outside the parameters of what is typically considered "church," and we were basically doing it based on our trust in God. We informed our denominational officials but sought nothing from them. They watched and waited to see what would happen, as we all did.

There was a real risk of failure and the repercussions that might come along with that, but I have to tell you that we really didn't think about that much at all. I was so convinced that God was leading us in a new direction that I didn't waste time worrying about what would happen if this "new thing" didn't work. Having the support of the leadership of St. Luke's—a congregation known for creative and leading-edge ministries—was invaluable! A new senior pastor willing to allow an associate pastor to "do her own thing" was another sign that we could and should step out and take the risk. It was by no means a sure thing, but with a lot of prayer and faith, we stepped out into an unknown future.

Doing a New Thing

In order to do a "new thing," we have to be ready to let go of the old. "Do not cling to events of the past, or dwell on what happened long ago," God says in Isaiah 43. Yet that is precisely what many congregations do. We hold up as sacred our creeds and hymns and styles of worship and never allow ourselves to see the possibility that there might be other ways to worship that can bring the worshiper into a close relationship with God. We close our minds and say, "That can't be church!" If it isn't what those of us who have always been a part of the church have come to expect, it must not be valid worship. Believe me! We have heard many comments like that, attacking what we're doing, calling it "unfaithful."

Allow me to share a story of something that happened during the first two years of The Garden's existence. Indianapolis was host to a United Methodist jurisdictional event on congregational development, and a group of the attendees elected to attend The Garden on Sunday morning. One gentleman, whose name I do not know, was very upset with what he experienced at our service and was apparently quite vocal. "How can you do what you're doing and call it church?"

A year or two later, the same man came up to me at another event in Cincinnati and shared what had happened to him after his visit to The Garden. He had been angry and upset by his experience, but he said to me, "One night God woke me up from a dead sleep,

11

saying to me, 'Who are you to decide how I reach my people?' " That was a life-changing moment for him. He began to understand that to limit God's reach through only one style of worship was limiting the limitless God. He began to be much more open to different ways of being church. I appreciated the man's honesty and his willingness to share the story with me, and I know that he was open to looking for God's activity in our world through a new set of eyes.

To do a "new thing," we have to be willing to look at our traditions, our liturgies, our hymns, and try to see them in a new way. What would someone who has never been to church understand about our worship? Would an outsider know the "password" or "secret handshake"? In today's world, the church is like a secret organization, and only the insiders know the language. Think about how hollow some of the words of our hymns can be to those who aren't familiar with them. Although "Holy, Holy, Holy" is one of my favorite hymns, I have to admit that I don't hear "which wert, and art, and evermore shall be" used much in everyday conversation. Ask someone what grace is, and we may hear that it's a prayer offered before a meal or someone's mother or the "grace period" on a bill. We often assume that everyone knows the Lord's Prayer or the Doxology or the Gloria Patria, but that is not true. Those outside the church simply do not understand some of our "churchy" language and seemingly obscure concepts.

I will spend more time later on the following issues, but in order to "do a new thing," we have to look at the blockades that those outside the church perceive. One of the things we hear about a church is, "All they ever talk about is money." It's important to consider financial stewardship as a vital part of our faith journey, while not turning off those who feel finances are a matter of private concern. Many have left the church because they felt they had to pay to stay, and their limited financial resources prevented their giving.

Another issue we have to consider is how we often create an insider-outsider atmosphere in our congregations. I sometimes visit a small-town church in Colorado, and one of the things that has happened during each visit is that the leader opens the floor to hear all the "joys and concerns" of the congregation. I hear about Aunt May's visit or Grandpa Joe's cancer. Although I care about those struggles and joys, hearing the regulars share their concerns excludes me and causes me to feel very much like a visitor. I also have a personal pet peeve and an intense dislike of "passing the peace" (time for greeting one another) in a service. To me, it feels forced and insincere, and I've found that most of the time people wind up talking with those they already know.

It's interesting to note that, during membership classes at St. Luke's, where there isn't that kind of greeting within the service and where we don't go rapping on doors soon after someone's visit to our church, people join because they appreciate being left alone. I have a friend in Kansas who has been looking for a new church home, and he has called us after each visit to talk about the cookies or loaf of bread he received. One arrived before he had even gotten home! I asked if he intended to go back to this church or that one, and his response each time was, "No, the service wasn't appealing enough for me to want to return, and I don't like to be smothered with attention." I know this flies in the face of some evangelism techniques, but I think we need to look long and hard at how we're conducting family insider business and pursuing our visitors with unwanted contacts.

Another turnoff for many people is the attire deemed appropriate for church. Frankly, I do not believe that God cares what we wear to church; some people may have an opinion on that issue, but God doesn't. Although many churches have become much more casual, that's certainly not true of all, and sometimes that can be an issue.

Walt Kallestad, whom I mentioned earlier, shared a story at a conference about trying to attend a church in Minnesota. He had gone out for an early morning walk and was dressed in shorts and a golf shirt. On his walk, he attempted to go into two different churches but was turned away because of how he was dressed. So much for open, loving, welcoming congregations! Suffice it to say that we must look at some of the blockades we create that keep people out.

Doing a "new thing" requires us to step out of the box and consider new ways of being church. Let me be clear on one thing: it is not about "dumbing down" the message or becoming "church lite." The message of the good news of God's unconditional love for us and presence with us never changes. The way in which we communicate the message is what changes. We have to think about the language we use to get the message across and the style of presentation, which I'll talk about in a later chapter.

Furthermore, it only takes a moment to look around and see what people experience in their everyday lives to know that we have to change our approach from the dull, boring, and routine style of worship to an experience that is filled with the vitality of the Spirit! Today people watch TV or go to concerts; and they get good music, good sound, good visual reinforcement; and that's what they've become accustomed to. Our mediocre, half-hearted efforts simply don't cut it in today's world. We have to be willing to realize that people receive a message in different ways, and we must alter our reliance on the spoken word that's offered without multisensory enhancement.

I believe that God is calling each of us to our own unique ministry. It is not a cookie-cutter cloned church, nor is it what has always been done. It is being willing to listen to God's voice and respond, stepping out in faith and confidence that we are living true to God's call.

Questions for Consideration

1. What new thing is God creating for you and your congregation?
2. How is God revealing that new thing to you? Can you see it?
3. Look at your setting with new eyes, and try to see what barriers you may be creating for those unfamiliar with the church.
4. How might you go about eliminating some of those barriers and blockades?
5. What is your basic attitude regarding reaching those who are outside the church? Upon what belief is that attitude based?
6. How would you describe your vision, passion, and call for ministry?

CHAPTER 3

PLANNING BEFORE PLANTING

From Vision to Reality

W hen I lead workshops on beginning a new ministry such as this one, my first point is plan, plan, plan. I cannot emphasize enough the importance of good planning to the success of any new endeavor; and it is vital to involve as broad a spectrum of planning or launch team persons as possible. Their involvement on the ground floor will help maintain a level of activity and enthusiasm and keep them actively involved in the process. Their key role builds ownership in the project and ensures their support, which is essential.

Having said that, however, I must add a caveat. We must take enough time to plan thoroughly and well, but not so much time that we lose energy and interest. The danger in any congregation is that a new idea gets talked to death and eventually dies from lack of air to breathe! Too much talking and bureaucratic decision-making red tape will suck the life out of a new endeavor and conceal anything God has in mind.

When we began The Garden in 1995, it was nearly eleven months from the dream in mid-November 1994 that gave birth to this satellite ministry until our first service. From mid-January until September 10, when we launched, we spent time planning, forming teams, studying, visiting, reading, envisioning what this would look like, and creating as much goodwill as possible. We wanted to foreclose on any possibility that lack of careful planning would jeopardize the future of The Garden.

An important part of the planning involves reading and researching what other churches and nonchurch organizations are doing. We visited Willow Creek, Community Church of Joy, and churches in our area who were trying a different style of worship, and we made those visits to find out what "felt" like us and what "felt" uncomfortable or unnatural to us. After each visit, our start-up team members would have lunch or dinner and process what we had experienced. What did we find appealing? How might we adapt this idea or that one to our setting? What failed to connect with us? What happened in this service that we would like to include in our setting? What do we *never* want to do?

I have to admit that I found books from disciplines other than the church much more helpful than any of those by our churched gurus, even the ones who were advocating new ways to worship. I've already mentioned the influence that Tom Peters's books had on me, but there were many others that I found extremely helpful at the beginning and yet others that have played a role in more recent times. A brief bibliography would include books such as *If It Ain't Broke, Break It!* (by Robert J. Kriegel and Louis Patler, Warner Books, 1991), *A Whack on the Side of the Head* (by Roger von Oech, Warner Books, 1998), *The Creative Spirit* (by Daniel Goleman, Paul Kaufman, and Michael Ray, Penguin Group, 1991), *Good to Great: Why Some Companies Make the Leap—and Others Don't* (by James Collins, HarperBusiness, 2001), *Gung Ho!* (by Kenneth Blanchard and Sheldon Bowles, Morrow, 1998), *Raving Fans* (by Kenneth Blanchard and Sheldon M. Bowles, Morrow, 1993), *Fish* (by Stephen C. Lundin, Harry Paul, and John Christensen, Hyperion, 2000), *Fish Tales* (by Stephen C. Lundin, John Christensen, and Harry Paul, Hyperion, 2002), and many others. Peruse the shelves of the library or bookstore, or browse Amazon.com to discover what the business world is reading, and take a look. Many new ways of working may emerge.

In the planning process, it is important to do the demographic and psychographic studies and research. To reach our target audience, it is vital that we know who they are, what they value, and what will attract and hold them. This isn't just something we find in reading *American Demographics* or in the U.S. census report. We have to get out into the community and get to know the people. What are they doing on Sunday mornings? What type of movies are they watching? Where do they eat? What is their favorite leisure time activity? What is the age group in a particular area? What is the educational level?

Much of this information is best gathered in a ministry of "hanging around." We have to go to the sporting events that everyone else is going to; it's important to become familiar with the favorite eating places, even if they are neighborhood pubs. Go on; it really won't hurt to walk in the door and get into a conversation with some of the folks. We might be amazed at what they would share and what we would learn about their lives and their struggles. Getting acquainted with the community can help us understand where the potential attendees are and what their needs are. This will move us miles forward when it comes to relating to them on Sunday morning.

Make a Ministry Plan

You may be asking yourself, "What's a ministry plan?" That's the very same question I asked when I was talking with my husband about this undertaking. He suggested that I write a "business plan," and I didn't know what that was. Fortunately, his MBA has not gone to waste, and he was able to describe for me the major points that should be included in any proposal for a new endeavor. The essential ingredients include the following:

- *What are our goals?* What are we hoping to achieve and accomplish? This becomes the basis for the vision statement of the ministry.
- *What are our objectives?* Objectives are always identifiable and measurable. For instance, what are our attendance goals? What revenue expectations do we have? This becomes the basis for our mission statement.
- *What is the service to be provided?* What will those who attend receive? Inspiration? Instruction? Celebration?

- *Who is the "target audience," and how will they be reached?*
  What type of individual are we trying to reach?
  Churched? Unchurched? Those in their twenties and
  thirties? What approaches will we use to let the ministry
  be known? What marketing appeal will get the word out?
- *How will this ministry be organized?* Who will lead us
  toward our goal, and how will we function? Top down?
  Teamwork?
- *How will it be financed?* What will it cost? Who will pay for
  it? What must the budget include?
- *What is the timetable for accomplishing the mission?* What do
  we plan to accomplish by when? When will information go
  out? When will the new ministry begin? When will the
  organizational structure be in place? What funds do we
  need to have in place, and by when?

You will find a copy of our original ministry plan in Appendix A
of this book. It might be helpful to peruse it before beginning to outline your own. Whatever path you choose, I encourage you to take
the time to plan as thoroughly and as carefully as possible, but please
be sure not to take so long that all energy for the ministry is lost!

Basic Decisions

There are some basic decisions that must be made at the outset.
For example, where will this ministry take place? Will it be housed in
the church building, or is it necessary to find another venue? This
was an easy issue for us to decide with The Garden because the
"mother" church, St. Luke's UMC, was "maxed out" in terms of facilities. There was simply no room on the church property for us to use.

We had to look for an alternative site to the church building, which
has turned out to be a blessing for a variety of reasons. For one thing,
we have been able to reach those who have been "turned out" or
"turned off" by past experiences with the church, and we have been
able to reach those who have had no prior connection with traditional
church. Many who attend The Garden would never darken the door
of a church building, feeling that they were not worthy enough or didn't

know the rituals. It can seem like alien territory to those who have no history with church, and those who have felt alienated for whatever reason can feel "safe" at an off-site location. In some cases, attendees are more comfortable in a more familiar setting, and this has allowed us to establish a trust relationship with our Gardeners.

For that reason alone, I'm relatively sure that The Garden will never build a church building. When we look for additional space, we always look at secular settings where the population goes for other events, and "Oh, by the way, this happens to house a church on Sundays." In addition, being free of maintaining a physical plant, of always worrying about bricks and mortar, allows us to focus on the ministry. I realize that the following statement may sound a bit callous, but if the roof of the theater or the banquet hall in which we meet springs a leak, it's not our issue.

Being off-site in borrowed or rented space has also been a definite advantage when it comes to launching a new enterprise. Just as the business world is discovering, it is much more cost-effective to lease or rent major items, rather than to tie up critical resources in real estate or soon-to-be-outdated equipment. This makes starting a new ministry a much more financially feasible undertaking.

Unlikely Partnerships

One of the pleasant surprises that has come as a result of our being an off-site entity is that we have been able to form some wonderful creative partnerships with other churches and with the business community. St. Luke's provides us with office space and pays the pastoral support items in our budget. The Garden pays the rest of its salaries, all programming costs, technical equipment, and all the materials and resources needed to do ministry. There have been partnerships that have provided mutual benefit to both St. Luke's and The Garden.

We have been able to establish good relationships with both Beef and Boards Theater and The Mansion at Oak Hill as a result of our being housed in their facilities. Again, both have benefited. Some come to our services and, as a result, think about The Mansion as a site for their wedding. Some who come to our services decide they will attend the Sunday matinee at the theater. Increased traffic means more visibility for both the business and the church. It's a win-win situation.

We have also been able to establish a good working partnership with our Annual Conference. The committee on new church development has been progressive and willing to assist with funding needs for satellite ministries, as well as the more traditional new church starts. As a result, they have given us grants for our unique marketing campaigns, for staffing, and most recently for launching our second site.

We are constantly exploring other possible partnerships and have had conversations with a variety of enterprises and foundations. Since we are heavily multimedia reliant, we have pursued the possibility of partnering with a company whose primary business is video and visual arts. We are in the process of working with a university to team with their communications department and Internet savvy to provide content for them. They have the technology and the funds, and we have the content they need. We have formed partnerships with community nonprofit agencies to help enhance their work. Suffice it to say that the opportunities for partnerships are limited only by our imaginations. We can do so much more together than any of us can do alone, and I think that's an important lesson for the church to learn.

A New Church Start, or What?

One of the questions we were often asked at the outset was, "Will this be a new church start?" Our response initially was, "We don't know. It depends on where God leads us." It seems to me that we in mainline denominations have to experience a paradigm shift when it comes to congregational development. Our model of buying a piece of property and assigning a pastor to start a church is an antiquated and ineffective model. That may have worked in the 1950s, but it hasn't worked well since. Of the most recent new church starts in our conference, only one is still "alive," but "alive" means a congregation of one hundred people. I'm certainly not trying to imply that more is better. However, it stuns me the amount of time, energy, and financial resources that have been expended to start a congregation of one hundred people—approximately four times the amount we have spent to launch a congregation of eight hundred people!

Part of the reason for The Garden's success is that we consider ourselves a "blossom" of St. Luke's United Methodist Church. St. Luke's is a large congregation with a vast array of ministries that meet a multitude of needs. St. Luke's regards The Garden as the "R and D" arm of the church, and that has allowed us to experiment with new approaches and radical ways of being "church." We took nothing away from the "big church" when The Garden was planted and have added an entirely new dimension to its ministry.

Furthermore, we do not have to reinvent the wheel. The ministries of St. Luke's have always been open to anyone in the community, and Gardeners are aware that they can take advantage of any and all offerings that St. Luke's has. At the same time, we have had the challenge of creating new ways of being church and coloring outside the lines. What does intergenerational worship really look like? What replaces the traditional Sunday school model? What would a youth ministry for the twenty-first century be like? What does an entirely different kind of organizational structure allow that the traditional church organization does not?

What I'm saying is that it's time for the mainline denominations to get outside the box and look at entirely new ways of being church. The methods we used to use are diminishing in effectiveness; and if current trends continue, the mainline church will be dead within this next century, and along with it, any positive effect and influence we might have on our world.

It's time to change things and consider new possibilities. Churches starting churches is one approach that works. Having a number of satellite communities attached to a solid "mother" church is another possibility. Encouraging large churches to share resources with smaller struggling churches is another option. For example, we could provide DVDs of the sermon or worship experience in an economical and effective way to other churches, and that enables those churches to offer meaningful worship without the expense of a retired, part-time, or student pastor. We could supply any church in our conference or beyond with a DVD of the message and music, and a worship leader in a local setting could provide the personal contact that each faith community needs. A student pastor or a retiree could provide the pastoral care in the course of the week, and could probably do that for four to six small churches. It seems to me that this is a much more viable way to enhance the ministry of our churches.

Denominational Connections

How has our conference of The United Methodist Church responded to The Garden? At first, it was definitely a wait-and-see attitude. Early on, we met with the Indianapolis district superintendents to share our intention to begin this new ministry, but we were clear with them that we were not seeking either permission or financial support. At the beginning, The Garden was seen as just another worship service that St. Luke's was starting. It was after this endeavor developed a positive track record that conference officials outwardly got aboard. They were always supportive in one-on-one conversations, but I suspect were tentative in conference gatherings.

After the first two to three years, it was smooth sailing. The bishop and cabinet have been very supportive of The Garden, and they have supported it not just in word, but with financial support, too. That relationship has been a positive one, and I see no reason that will not continue into the future.

Questions for Consideration

1. What steps should your congregation take to be ready to launch a new ministry? What research? Where will you visit?
2. What are potential partnerships that could be formed to create this new undertaking?
3. What is your congregation's relationship to judicatory officials, and how might this be a win-win for your situation?
4. What would your ministry plan look like, and how would it help develop both a vision and a mission statement for your church?

CHAPTER 4

LAYING OUT THE GARDEN

J ust as any gardener decides what he or she is going to plant in the garden and where each flower or vegetable will go, so, too, must we think in the same way in planting a new ministry. This chapter will describe some of the preliminary thinking that must take place for any new endeavor to succeed. There are some essential first steps and some "nuts and bolts" things that need to be in place before launching a new ministry such as The Garden and some basic questions that must be asked, and answered.

Influencing the Church's Leadership

Fortunately, this was not a difficult thing at St. Luke's, because this congregation has a long history of empowering lay and clergy alike to follow their passion. We tried to communicate the vision to our key leaders in informal ways. For instance, the first time that the six or seven key persons heard about this new thing was at a breakfast gathering. I had asked several of them to meet me for breakfast so that we could discuss a new ministry for St. Luke's; and typical of their commitment to trying to be the best we could be, they were wholeheartedly in support of the idea. It would have been difficult for them not to be. It wasn't really going to affect anything at the home site; nothing would be changed there. This would simply be an "added value" for St. Luke's, which is well known in the Indianapolis community as a forward-thinking, progressive church.

It also helped that I had been a part of that congregation for so many years and a part of a trusted clergy team. People knew me, and we could build on relationships.

I suspect, at the beginning, that there was some fear that this new thing would draw people away from St. Luke's, but we tried to be very clear that we were not trying to compete with what was happening there. Instead, we were trying to reach a whole new group of people with an entirely different approach. That proved to be exactly what happened. Sure, some folks from St. Luke's began to attend The Garden, but St. Luke's sanctuary was always more than full to overflowing every Sunday. Actually, we helped open up some space that allowed for the home congregation to continue growing, even while planning and building a new sanctuary and other additional ministry space.

One other element must be noted here, and that is that we never actually asked for board or committee approval to start what became The Garden. St. Luke's has long operated in the style of "seek forgiveness, not permission." Staff and laity alike have always been encouraged to follow their passion, and if that means a new ministry, then recruit others to follow, and go for it! That's exactly what happened with The Garden. We announced to the administrative board that this venture was going to happen, but we never asked for an OK. Even if we had, I'm certain the answer would still have been a resounding yes because that's just the way St. Luke's is.

In communicating this idea to the conference, we had conversations with our denominational officials, but, again, not to ask for anything from them. We met with the two Indianapolis district superintendents and the head of the metropolitan mission group to let them know what we were planning, but we were not seeking their permission. To them, at least initially, I suspect this notion of going off-site and doing some weird thing seemed relatively harmless; and if this big congregation wanted to support it, so much the better. That lack of interest or involvement didn't last long, however. As the endeavor gained momentum, others came to learn from us, and the district and conference endorsed our ministry wholeheartedly.

Name and Place

What will we call this undertaking? When we first began what is now called The Garden, we began with the ministry plan outlined in the previous chapter. Then my first "official" meeting was with three people who were members of St. Luke's and professionals in the field of marketing. I explained the concept, shared the ministry plan, and talked about the fact that we did not necessarily want to include the word *church* in the name; nor did we have strong feelings about identifying ourselves with The United Methodist Church. This was not a statement against United Methodism, but rather an acknowledgment of the fact that demographic studies pointed out that those outside the church were not attracted to any particular denominational affiliation. That simply is not a matter of appeal for many in our population today.

Those three marketing professionals went away after our meeting, and I next heard from them several weeks later when one arranged a time to meet with me. He arrived with a design of a logo, and the name—The Garden, *A Blossom of St. Luke's United Methodist Church*. To be honest, that was my only moment of real doubt that we were heading in the right direction. You see, anyone who knows me knows better than to give me a living plant because I can kill it in a matter of days. My dad was a master gardener, but I have not inherited his passion for growing things or his talent. I thought God was trying to play some huge joke on me, saying, "Linda, you only think this is what I want you to do. Think again."

And yet, I respected the work of these professionals and wanted to honor their involvement. Our next step was to present it to the core of folks who had expressed an interest in joining in on the launch. They, too, responded in a sort of lukewarm fashion, but they also pointed out how rich the image of a garden is, and how the ideas for marketing campaigns could build on that theme that is firmly based in biblical tradition. The name caught on, and today, I can't imagine it being called anything else. It seems that God was right after all, and we got into the garden image, even to the point of describing ourselves as an organic entity that grows and thrives in God's own time.

Resources

Considering how The Garden got its name reminds me that I should address the topic of the resources each of our congregations has that typically go untapped. I know of few churches that do not have someone with rich life and work experience who can offer volumes of expertise in a variety of fields. Seldom do we in the church use wisely the amazing talent that many of our parishioners demonstrate in their chosen field of endeavor.

For us, this began with the marketing gurus who were a part of St. Luke's. Although your congregation might not have marketing talent, my guess is that there is someone in your community or nearby who would willingly share some time and basic information that could point a church in the right direction. I would suggest finding those who have expertise in the field of marketing, and pick their brains. Those who know the context of the community, and who make their living trying to get the attention of that community, will have a great deal of wisdom to share when it comes to knowing what name might appeal to folks who are not a part of traditional church, if that group is our "target" group. What image represents the type of ministry we are in the process of creating? What "product branding" would make us known in a region? They know, and I suspect all we need to do is ask for their input, and this applies to virtually every area of church life, not just to marketing efforts.

Location

I've already talked about the fact that there was simply no space at St. Luke's for us to conduct this ministry, but that has turned out to be an immense advantage. Although most churches probably don't encounter that situation, I would still encourage churches to be creative when it comes to the space for a new ministry. It is much more financially feasible to use space that already exists, and which might be available for church use on Sunday mornings. The possibilities are endless: movie theaters, school auditoriums, condominium clubhouses, office buildings, the YMCA or YWCA, and even enterprises such as a bar or restaurant often have space availability during their off-peak hours.

In my opinion, any space that is chosen, whether it is in the church building itself or elsewhere, must provide a comfortable welcoming environment for those who attend. One of the surprises we encountered was that at both of our sites, people sit around tables. I had always thought of tables as barriers to communication, but I have been proved wrong. People who gather around tables form instant community, and tables create a more informal atmosphere for newcomers. Tables encourage connection and relationship, and that, for me, is much of what our faith is all about—building relationships with God and with others. I'd urge anyone considering the possibility of designing an experience to attract the "unchurched" to consider the use of tables and chairs or even comfortable couches and chairs (although that set-up could possibly limit capacity). They offer a less intimidating, more welcoming setting.

Start with a Core

I cannot emphasize too much the importance of beginning with a core of people. We asked people from St. Luke's to commit to spend one year with us to help us get started and "pad" the crowd. About seventy-five responded to the call, and their help was invaluable! They became part of the various teams that moved this from an abstract concept to a concrete reality. I will discuss how this unfolded in chapter 6.

When we began, our goal was to have 200 in attendance at the first service, and we had 202. That was mainly because this core group of 75 believed in what we were doing. They spread the word, and they were the hands and hearts that formed the spirit of this new ministry. After the first year, some returned to St. Luke's, but many remained to provide support on a regular or occasional basis; and their encouragement and appreciation of the core that began The Garden has never wavered.

Questions for Consideration

1. What critical decisions must we make in order to move forward in this new endeavor?
2. How are we going to mobilize to launch this new ministry? Who will lead? Who will follow? How do we make it happen?
3. Write down the next three most important steps you need to take to bring about this "new thing."

CHAPTER 5

WORKING TOGETHER IN THE GARDEN

The organization of The Garden is definitely built on teamwork. Admittedly, it is often hard work and takes a great
deal more time and effort than going it on our own.
However, I'm convinced that it is the only way to be in ministry
today. The rewards far exceed the demands of the work and are seen
in the final product, whether that is a Sunday service, a special
event, or budget planning for the year. In essence, the whole is
always greater than the sum of its parts.

I suppose that, to a great extent, my commitment to team ministry has come out of my work as a layperson in a congregation, as
well as the gift I have had of working with a very talented clergy
team. In my early days of ordained ministry, I was fortunate to find
myself in a mix with five other very different, yet highly gifted and
committed, clergypersons. I was always included, and the mentoring
often happened by dropping into one another's offices and chatting
or by an informal lunch or by a raucous gathering over a glass of wine
and dinner. We worked hard, and we worked together. We loved one
another dearly, and we sometimes argued vehemently with one
another. Nonetheless, our commitment to one another, to the team
process, and to the well-being of our congregation were never in
question. Because of that experience, for which I will be forever
grateful, I am deeply committed to working as a team to accomplish
whatever mission has been set out for us.

Although the active teams always seem to be a moving target, there are approximately eighteen different teams who are doing the work of The Garden at any given time. They consist of the following: Leadership Team, Lead Team, Worship Design Team, Music Teams, Video Team, Message Team, Communication Team, Development Team, Marketing Team, Prayer Team, Hospitality Teams (I'll explain how they organize and work later), Tech Team, Garden Kids Lead Team, Garden Youth Team, Outreach Team, Comfort and Care Team, Creative Team, and various teams that meet on a short-term basis for special projects, for example, a launch team and a renewal leave team. Each team has its own team leader who coordinates gatherings, trains new team members, and makes sure important information is shared by all team members.

To give you an illustration of how we try to function, let me say a bit about how our Worship Design Team works. The work for any given Sunday begins months prior when the Message Team gets together to choose and schedule upcoming themes. This team tries to keep a finger on the pulse of the congregation and to be aware of what's happening in our city and world that affects our Gardeners. In other words, they generally bring to the meeting ideas of "felt needs" among our population. This group suggests titles and outlines the themes for Sundays three to six months in advance.

Their work is then handed off to the Worship Design Team, which meets every Tuesday evening from 6:00 P.M. to 8:00 P.M. It typically is comprised of the pastor, the creative director, and eight to ten others, some of whom represent special areas of consideration for worship. The goal of each Tuesday is to gather ideas for upcoming Sundays, to fine-tune all the details for the next service, and to create the "flow" for the service that is ten days away. During meetings, we brainstorm how to make future services meaningful and relevant and try to identify the creative ideas that might require additional time and energy from our volunteers to make them happen. The speaker usually shares potential stories, anecdotes, and quotes that might be used in the spoken message; and other team members contribute personal stories, opinions, or other ideas that might have an influence on the ultimate outcome of the speaker's message. We also share any ideas for special videos, handouts, or activities that we might want to include in a particular service.

When the time comes to focus on the two Sundays immediately ahead, the assumption is that every team member has read the message that came to them several weeks earlier by e-mail, and they're prepared to help us tie everything together into a meaningful whole. We hear the lyrics of the songs that are suggested, and we view the movie clips or original videos from which we will select those that ultimately will be a part of the service. Eventually, through a process we've come to call "Creative Collaborative Chaos," order reigns, and a service flow is set. It's been very much a team process, with everyone giving their input, and having been heard, working together to create the very best service we can craft.

I will talk more later about the shift this style of working requires from the pastoral leader, and it may well be dramatic for some. We all probably know preachers who refuse to share their sermon prior to the moment it is preached. Many actually create the sermon "on the fly" or, at best, the night before. One thing that is required for good teamwork is that each team member does his or her part, and that includes the preacher. It is not possible to provide a quality service with last-minute work. Because I want to honor the time commitment our many volunteers are giving to this ministry, I make sure that my messages are done and e-mailed to all team members at least three and preferably four weeks in advance. I will discuss the process that works for me in a later chapter.

It seems to me that the benefits of teamwork far outweigh the disadvantages. For one thing, we pastors don't have to carry the whole weight of the worship experience on our shoulders. Other team members are so deeply invested in the process and in the service itself that they, too, receive the good feeling that comes from working together to create something that has touched others at the heart of their being.

Frankly, another plus to teamwork is that none of us as pastors, no matter how gifted we think we are, can do it all. When we try to play the Lone Ranger role, I think we're depriving our laypersons of a wonderful opportunity for them to discover new talents and interests and to blossom and bloom on their own. We're robbing them of these opportunities if we attempt to stay high on our pedestal and keep it all to ourselves, and I personally feel that we are failing to be the church as it was intended to be.

It is truly exciting to witness the awakening of passion within new team members, to equip and empower them, and then to watch what happens. It's important to give folks the responsibility for their work and then to show appreciation for what they have done, along with offering counsel or guidance when things don't go as planned.

There's one other essential ingredient in teamwork, and that is this: Teams are built on relationship, a relationship of trust—trust of one another and deep trust in the God who has called us to work together. That means that there will be times when we are vulnerable; there will be times that we have to move over to cover when someone is hurting; there will be times when we have to give more than we think we can; there will be times when we have to let go of our control needs, and there will be times when we're irritated with one another. Teamwork encompasses the full gamut of human emotions, including an intense joy and camaraderie that can't be found any other way.

It always means that we respect and honor our team members. I fear that the church has often abused and misused our valued lay members by not honoring them and the most valuable commodity we all possess—our time. I sometimes struggle with that after a frustrating team meeting in which it seems as though we've gone around in circles and wasted our time. I believe it is extremely important for the key leaders to do their best to make sure all gatherings are needed and productive; it is equally important that team gathering be times of spiritual growth and sharing our cares and concerns for one another. The leadership definitely sets the tone, and it behooves each of us who call ourselves leaders to come to our team meetings in the most positive spirit possible. If we don't take the lead in that, team members will become disillusioned, feel disempowered, and eventually disappear.

Another way we value them is by making sure they have the gifts and desire to do what we're asking them to do. I'm convinced that one of the greatest gifts we can give others is helping them discover what they're good at, and then giving them the opportunity to take the ball and run with it. We can't try to control every situation, but we have to honor and trust that they will do what they have committed to do.

The best part of teamwork is the fun we have doing the work. "Many hands make light work" may not always be true in teamwork; but the gift of time spent together, laughter and comfort shared, and a job well done can't be beat! I definitely advocate looking into this way of "doing ministry." It's fulfilling and delightful!

Questions for Consideration

1. If your congregation expressed interest in becoming more team oriented in its work, where would you begin?
2. What resistance to teamwork exists? How do you begin to deal with that?
3. What changes will the pastor have to undergo to be an effective team leader or team member?
4. Who could assist your congregation in reorganizing around effective teamwork?

CHAPTER 6

PLANTING SEEDS

Who Is the "Target Audience"?

One thing we were clear about when this new endeavor began to unfold was that we wanted to reach new people. We described them as "unchurched," a term I now hesitate to use since some find that term derogatory and demeaning. Yet it is often how we refer to those who have never attended church, or it has been years since they've darkened the door of a church.

I prefer to say that our goal has always been to reach those who haven't, for whatever reason, heard and received the message of God's unconditional love. That group may be folks who have sat in churches for many years, but the conventional way of sharing the good news never got through. That collection of people could be those who have been turned out or turned off by traditional church, and it could also pertain to those who have never been part of a church in any way, shape, or form.

We did our homework, which consisted in part of demographic profiles of the northwest Indianapolis area. Studies showed that more than half of the population within a five-mile radius of our initial site (the dinner theater) qualified as "unchurched," that is, they had not been to a church except perhaps for a wedding or funeral within the last six months to one year. That was the segment of the population we wanted to reach.

More specifically, because most of the leadership that was emerging was of the baby boomer generation, we said we wanted to reach unchurched boomers. A friend who was in the doctoral program with me at the time that The Garden was a seedling gave me some of the best counsel I received at that very formative stage. He said, "Be careful, Linda, how tightly you draw your target. See who you get, and then draw your target around them." Sure enough, he was absolutely right!

We certainly attracted and continue to attract a large number of baby boomers, but those who responded to our appeal came from a much larger part of the population than we ever imagined possible. The Garden today is a diverse collection of people. It includes everyone from preschoolers to retirees, and they represent every aspect of the wider population in race, color, ethnicity, education, and economic backgrounds. They are gay and straight, married and single, men and women, boys and girls, young and old, wealthy and poor, professionals and jobless; every spectrum is represented among our Gardeners, and that has produced a richness that we could never have experienced had we drawn only unchurched boomers.

My counsel to those who are considering such a ministry is the same as that of my friend. On the one hand, be very clear about who you are and who you want to reach. On the other hand, be ready for surprises, and respond accordingly.

How Do We Gather the Core with Whom We Start?

We began with those we knew and had lunches and endless conversations with them, explaining what we were about, and asking if they had any interest in joining us for a year to be pioneers in a whole new venture. This approach produced lots of yeses. That wasn't our only approach, however. We put announcements in the St. Luke's bulletin and newsletter and invited anyone who was interested in helping to come to an informational meeting. Each of the two times those meetings were held, we had approximately thirty-five to forty in attendance. Again, we presented the vision and idea and shared an example of what we hoped this new thing would be and enlisted their help and their support. Almost everyone was willing to give us one year to launch this yet-unnamed entity.

As the planning moved forward, this is the group that began visiting Willow Creek and other churches who were doing "contemporary" worship. We read several books and articles, but the most helpful in forming what Sunday mornings would look like was a book by Tim Wright entitled *A Community of Joy*. That book and the Community Church of Joy's evangelism conference were influential in what we eventually became. We certainly don't "do" worship the way Joy does; we benefited from their work because they knew the right topics to cover and the right questions to ask. They still do and offer wonderful resources to those looking to try something different.

After the first couple months of visiting and research, we began to form some of the basic teams we would need to plant this thing that was to be called The Garden. We knew we wanted to welcome people as warmly as we could, and that would require hospitality; so those who had a propensity toward that kind of ministry migrated toward that team. This included greeters in the parking lot, as well as those who would set up the food we planned to serve during the service. We knew we wanted worship to be far different from anything we had experienced before, so those who wanted to envision what that might be like moved into that area. This group included a young woman who has been vital to the shape of The Garden because she loves movies and can remember every scene in every movie! What an unexpected find!

Some expressed an interest in technology and how it could enhance what we were doing, and they began to form themselves into a team to investigate and make recommendations about our needs. I knew we wanted to reach people in a whole new way, and that meant marketing. A dozen or so persons expressed interest in that arena, and our marketing team was launched.

At that point, I was interested in the meta model of ministry and felt that small groups were the way to go. Eight others indicated a similar interest, and our "ministry team," or small group leaders, got involved in a training module to prepare themselves. Since children's ministry runs concurrently with worship at St. Luke's, I assumed the same thing would happen at The Garden. Someone stepped forward to head up a team to create a children's ministry. Of course, we didn't know yet that both kids and parents wanted to stay together in worship rather than be split apart. Those were the teams that were formed at the start, and most of them still exist, albeit in a mutated form.

Be Clear on What You Are About

It is important to talk through and make critical decisions early on in the process of planning a new endeavor. There are some basic decisions that must be made before one can proceed with planning and implementing the plan. What is our purpose in beginning this ministry? Are we trying to change the whole congregation, a segment of it; or is this an outreach ministry, a mission?

Typically, a new thing is regarded with some suspicion by most congregations. There is always the fear that they are going to lose something, so I think it is important to be clear that we are not taking anything away from the existing church situation. In other words, they don't have to go through a grieving process or become angry because their favorite hymns are no longer being sung. Our answer, it seems to me, must always be, "Yes, and ..." It is both/and, and not either/or.

I've seen many congregations get in trouble when they force people to change. Most of us realize how difficult change is when we *want* to change, and we are faced daily with a rapidly changing world. How can we do both? How can we reach new people yet continue to feed and nourish those who have long been a part of our congregation? It's a sensitive issue, and one must proceed cautiously. However, I think it is most helpful if the leadership is very clear on the purpose for this new undertaking and is open with the rest of the congregation.

Discover What You Do Well

An important consideration for a new ministry is to determine its strengths. It is important to determine what we do well and to do it to the very best of our ability. As strange as it may seem, we don't do much drama at The Garden at Beef and Boards, and we're in a working Actors Equity dinner theater! We have some of the gifts that are needed to do drama, but we have found that we cannot do it well on a consistent basis; and we have elected to go with more video than live drama sketches. That's because we have a talented video guru who has a wonderful eye for creating just the right original piece that ties closely with our theme for the day. Not everyone has the bene-fit of such talent, but we all have some talents that are better than others. If we focus on those strengths and work to improve them, our ministry will take a big step toward succeeding.

There's something else about focusing on our strengths, too. If we do what we do best, that produces a level of quality that we can't get any other way. And if we focus on quality and striving toward excel-lence, we typically get it. Incidentally, there's a strange reality that goes along with this: talent matters, and quality attracts quality. Along with affirming that we need to focus on what we do well comes an accompanying caution: "If you can't do something well, don't do it."

I'm certainly not talking about perfection, but there's nothing in today's world that puts people off more than poor presentations. A drama sketch poorly done is painful, both for the presenters and for the congre-gation. Music that is flat or poorly sung is an embarrassment for every-one. I believe that it is important to maximize those things at which we are good and minimize those at which we are less than adequate.

Decide to Be Authentic

Another commitment that any new ministry must make is to be authentic. There's no point in trying to copy exactly what someone else is doing, because it comes across as less than real, less than gen-uine. I've seen many instances in which a church tries to do exactly the same thing some other congregation does, and it usually fails miserably. That's because it doesn't necessarily fit in with the con-text in which we're doing ministry.

Authenticity is something that people instinctively sense, and although they may not be able to articulate it clearly, I really believe that most folks are looking for what's real, authentic, sincere, and from the heart. For our own integrity, it's vital that we be ourselves and not try to be someone else—The Garden, Willow Creek, Saddleback, or any other church we might happen to admire.

Think About Participation in Worship

It is important to think through what constitutes participation in the worship experience. As mentioned earlier, we do not use praise music during our service, so the typical participation technique in contemporary services of having people stand up and sing endless verses together is not what we do. I won't go into all the reasons we have chosen not to sing praise choruses, but in a nutshell, it's because of the theology and the lyrics that do not use inclusive language in reference to God or human beings.

However, one of the things we have learned is that it is possible, and perhaps even preferable, to engage the attendee's heart instead of focusing on active participation that everyone does together. One of the things each of us must decide is what actually constitutes a meaningful worship experience for those who come.

What is it that connects most with worshipers? Is it singing together or reciting a creed or prayer together? Is it engagement? What about laughter and applause? To reach new populations of people, we may need to redefine what participation during worship is for us.

That means that we may need to reexamine our understanding of worship. Why do we gather to worship? Are we offering inspiration, or are we there to celebrate? Is this to be a teaching time, or do we need to engage in correcting those who've gone astray? How do we want people to feel when they leave our service? Encouraged? Hopeful? Reprimanded? Admonished?

We really must make some conscious decisions about the goal of worship, and not assume that what has always been will always be. At The Garden, we say that our worship experience is created for celebration and inspiration. We do not use that time for intentional instructional purposes, although clearly some learning takes place. Our desire is for people to leave the service with the conviction that God loves them and that they can make it through the week. We want them to laugh and find hope in our experience and to find confidence that they are not alone as they walk through the days ahead. That's what we have decided, but it's up to each of us to decide for ourselves. What do we need from our worship experience that will make a difference in our lives?

Copyrights and Licensing

With so much information available on the Internet, the issue of copyright and licensing seems to be a "moving target" these days. Since we tend to use secular music and contemporary movie clips, we have tried to be certain that we operate totally within the legal boundaries in order to keep from infringing on another's copyrighted material. I urge each congregation that offers a nontraditional service to research the current understanding about copyrighted material and adhere to the restrictions.

Having said that, I also want to add that, over the years, licenses have become available that allow congregations to use both contemporary Christian music and current movie clips during a service. The cost is nominal, and the guidelines are very clear. We are always conscious of running the various license numbers in our program each and every week.

This can be a time-consuming task, especially amid the heavy demands of creating a new way to worship. However, it is important to comply with the law by securing the necessary permission and licenses. It is helpful for a congregation to designate someone (as we designate our creative director) to be current in his or her understanding of copyright rules and regulations.

Questions for Consideration

1. Who will be the target audience for the new ministry?
2. If you decide that starting with a core group is a good idea, how will you, in your context, find those willing to help?
3. What is your purpose in starting this new ministry? Articulate it clearly and succinctly.
4. Assess the strengths that each person brings to this undertaking. What are they? How can they be best used?
5. What does it mean for you and your team to be authentic and real?
6. Explore your understanding of the purpose of worship.

CHAPTER 7

THE CLIMATE

Any gardener knows the importance of climate on the harvest. If favorable conditions don't prevail, flowers and vegetables fail to thrive, and our end result is not what we wanted or hoped for. In much the same way, the environment we create for our ministry is important when it comes to shaping the kind of ministry that is eventually harvested.

Before we actually began The Garden, the newly formed teams started to visualize what they wanted to have happen as people arrived at the dinner theater-turned-church. What would it "feel" like? What would it look like? We quickly realized that the parking lot is where it all starts, and a couple stepped forward to be parking lot greeters. They have been the most loyal Gardeners, are seldom absent, and start the spirit of warmth and welcome that continues, hopefully, throughout the morning. Our second site began with the very same assumption: it makes people feel welcomed to be greeted when they arrive in the parking lot, and often it helps them find a parking space.

Once attendees are parked and ready to enter the building, they are greeted at the front door by someone handing out programs and, once inside the theater itself, are directed by signage and by Gardeners to food tables and assisted in finding seats, if that is necessary. That process is the same at both sites, but the two venues are actually quite different.

Both of our sites are places of business—a professional dinner theater and a banquet hall. Each offers a set of strengths and some

limitations. At the theater, we benefit from the thrust stage, professional lighting and sound, and the expertise of several very talented
persons who know how to use this environment to its best advantage. Guests at the theater are seated around different-sized tables in
a darkened, semicircular, tiered setting.

To create and maintain the comfort level that begins with people
seated around a table, we have chosen to serve food during the service. We offer bagels, doughnuts, muffins, juice, and coffee during
the services; and people are very comfortable getting up to refill a
cup of coffee or get another plate of food while the band is playing
or the message is being given. This is easily accomplished since there
are no people seated in pews to climb over. The darkened atmosphere also serves to make the movement virtually unnoticeable.

The banquet hall is significantly different in "feel" from the theater. Lighting is an issue there, since it has three walls of windows
looking out on fifty-four glorious wooded acres! However, because
we are dependent on visual reinforcement for our services, the blinds
are pulled at the very beginning of the service to enhance the quality of the visuals on the screens and are raised as soon as the service
is completed. At the banquet facility, all the tables are round and
seat eight persons. There is more instant community built as people
sit together and can actually see one another considerably better
than at Beef and Boards. This venue also serves food and drink in
the same manner that the theater does.

Why did we choose to serve food during the service instead of at
the "fellowship" time afterward or between services? For one thing,
we operate under time restraints at both sites, and there isn't a great
deal of time for socializing in the theater or the hall immediately
after the services. More important, however, was trying to provide as
comfortable and "safe" a setting as we possibly could. Food provides
comfort and helps people feel more relaxed and at ease. Eating during the service also breaks through the typical church prohibition of
"No food or drink in the sanctuary!" That helps establish our
counter–church culture.

Recorded music plays as people enter both sites. We have tried to
match the music with the day's theme, but that has not always been
successful. Often we play one of our band's CDs or an instrumental
or a piano CD. It is never "church music." Our theory is that we

want people to hear the same music they just heard on their car radio on the drive there; and since one of the top stations in our city is the light rock station, that tends to be the type of music we use during the service.

We often talk about what it looks like to "lower the threshold." In other words, what can we do to remove the blockades that many experience when they go to church? We also use the term "no prior experience required" to describe the basic philosophy of our worship experience. No one needs to know when to sit or stand, because we don't do that; no one needs to know the Lord's Prayer or any other standard element of worship, because if we use any of them, the words are always on screen. The movie clips and popular music we use attempt to create a common bond by building on the familiar and by blurring the lines that are typically drawn between the sacred and the secular.

I cannot emphasize enough the importance of hospitality. It is the responsibility of every one of us to set the tone of informality, warmth, and friendliness, without becoming intrusive or offensive. Having said that, however, it is important to note how vital our hospitality teams are to fostering the environment that we want to create. We have separate hospitality teams for every service each Sunday of the month and team leaders who are responsible for making sure their team members know their roles and carry them out. Their work begins early on Sunday with setting up the food tables, picking up and distributing the food, setting up the information tables, putting pertinent information on the tables, preparing any handouts for the end of the service, and generally attending to all the details surrounding the service.

Their work is not done once the service ends. Everything has to be loaded for storage in the limited space we have at both sites or loaded for transport back to St. Luke's where we store music stands, amps, and so on. In addition, at Beef and Boards, we vacuum the floors, clear the lobby, clean the restrooms, polish the glass top tables, and help the wait staff put ice and water in the glasses for the incoming matinee audience. (Incidentally, the doors for the matinee open forty-five minutes after our last service finishes, so it is a hustle.)

We try to respect the desire some have to remain anonymous. That means, unless an attendee checks yes in response to the question, "May we contact you?" which is at the bottom of the comment card on every table each week, we do not make contact other than during the service. I often say it is important that our hospitality is welcoming, but not smothering. We do not single out newcomers, nor do we pursue them. We want to respect their rights as individuals to make the choice to return and to become known. As a result, we sometimes have those who attend for a year or more before they feel comfortable enough to make themselves known to us.

There are a couple of other blockades that we have tried to eliminate, or at least to minimize. One is attire. I don't think it matters to God what we wear when we come to church, and therefore, we don't care how one is dressed at The Garden. We have our Harley riders who come in their leathers, our golfers ready to head out to the golf course, and our Colts or Pacers fans arriving in their game wear. Many people wear jeans or shorts, while others choose to wear business casual attire. It makes no difference to us; we just want people to be comfortable so they can be open for connection with God.

I have concerns about the many congregations that conduct what I call "family business." That is the tradition of making announcements or sharing the "joys and concerns" that are usually "insider" news. They are mostly irrelevant to the newcomer and tend to create more of an insider/outsider situation. It might be better to find ways to communicate the pertinent information other than spoken announcements. We run the announcements on screen before each service begins, and they're also in the program and on our Web site. I realize that there are times when announcements cannot be avoided, but they should be brief and not allowed to disrupt the flow and sense of worship.

Another blockade to church for many is money. How many times have we heard, "All they ever talk about is money"? Or, "All they want is my money. They don't care about me." Obviously, money is one taboo topic in our society, and we walk a tightrope at The Garden. We have decided not to ask for money during the worship service; and when our theme is around our financial resources, we typically talk about the relationship between our faith and our money. However, we try to do it in a way that allows Gardeners to reflect and ponder the matter in their hearts to determine what that means for them.

However, it is clear that every ministry needs money to support its work and outreach. We have chosen to put watering cans at the doors, money envelopes on the tables, and announcements on screen regarding how to give to The Garden. We also try to keep current financial data on the information tables so those who wish can be better informed about where our money comes from and what our expenses are. Again, this will be discussed more thoroughly in chapter 11, the chapter on financing The Garden.

Let me reiterate some of the elements I believe to be necessary to make worship as inviting as possible.

- Parking lot helpers: It all starts in the parking lot to provide a warm, welcoming, friendly, and helpful beginning to the experience.
- Greeting and gathering: It is important to have greeters at the doors to welcome everyone again and to assist newcomers in knowing the ropes, in finding the food, and in finding a place to sit. It also creates a spirit of warmth to have hospitality team members or service participants wander around to the tables to chat with Gardeners and to meet newcomers.
- Signage: We use signs outside to help people find The Garden. Someone transports, places, and removes the signs each week. There is also signage inside showing where the food is and service times. I find it hard to have too many signs helping visitors find their way, no matter what our setting is.
- Establishing a comfort level: Music playing as people enter can help create a more welcoming presence, and controlled lighting can offer both warmth and anonymity, if desired. It's advantageous to have something on screen to watch or a program to read. Food and drink can break the ice and provide attendees opportunities to become acquainted with one another.
- "No prior experience required": Assume that the people who come are totally unfamiliar with church, and create

a level playing field. It's important to make sure there aren't foreign phrases spoken or printed—such as "UMW." Explain that UMW stands for United Methodist Women. We need to look at our language and expressions with a new eye and make all information as clear as possible.

- Multisensory: We try to do something each Sunday that appeals to all the senses, although the sense of smell can be a tough one. We also like to use humor to break down the walls that can separate us but try to be careful that it's not insider humor. We also find that we need to be aware of music and videos that appeal to both the children and elders who are present.
- Blending of sacred and secular: Our belief is that God is in everything and everything is in God. Therefore, we try to live out our conviction that there is no separation between the sacred and secular. We use secular music, put it in a different context, and find that it takes on an entirely new meaning.
- Contacting: We do not visit in homes or invade a person's privacy unless we are invited or told it is OK. We do have a packet of information that we can give or send to newcomers if they express an interest in learning more about The Garden. If, on our comment cards, they say it is permissible to contact them, we make a phone call within the next day or two, assessing how we can provide more information or be of any other assistance.
- Worship program: Our program is really more like a playbill and does not contain an "order of worship." It lists the announcements, has the Bible passage in it (note that we use words "Bible passage" rather than "Scripture," again, assuming nothing), the day's theme, and the names of the Hospitality Team, Tech Team, and participants in today's service.
- "Coloring outside the lines": It's important to remember that the message is eternal; it's the method of sharing the message that changes. It's important to look at the language we use and try to use plain, common, ordinary

everyday words, and not "church-ese," to convey the message. The goal is to communicate, and that means people can receive the message. Let's define our terms, not use churchy talk, and realize that getting the message across most often requires visual reinforcement and a multisensory approach.

As we think about reaching out to share the message of God's unconditional love and grace, I believe that we are trying to be true to the Great Commission. Remember the words Jesus shared with his disciples: "I have been given all authority in heaven and on earth. Go, then, to all peoples everywhere and make them my disciples: baptize them in the name of the Father, the Son, and the Holy Spirit, and teach them to obey everything I have commanded you. And I will be with you always, to the end of the age" (Matthew 28:18-20).

Jesus said, "Go, then, to all peoples everywhere." That means that we need to go the extra mile, removing the impediments to relationship with God, and reaching out in whatever ways we can to share this timeless message.

Questions for Consideration

1. What barriers have you perhaps unknowingly set up to outsiders? How might you go about lowering those barriers? How willing are you to do that?
2. What might make your worship experience more hospitable?
3. Think about your understanding of the relationship between the sacred and the secular. Is there a gap between the two? If so, how wide is the gap, and how might you narrow it (should you choose to do so)?
4. What is your basic attitude regarding reaching those who are unchurched? Upon what belief is your attitude based?

CHAPTER 8

PLANTING THE BASICS

"Make a careful exploration of who you are and the work you have been given, and then sink yourself into that. Don't be impressed with yourself. Don't compare yourself with others. Each of you must take responsibility for doing the creative best you can with your own life."
Galatians 6:4-5 (Message)

Creating worship is basic to who we are as the church, and it is important to be clear on the theology upon which we build worship and how our theology influences and permeates the message we convey. For those of us at The Garden, we believe God accepts, loves, and forgives each one of us, and we want to model that. We attempt to convey that message in everything we say and do. In fact, it is our theology that undergirds our mission, which is stated as follows: "The mission of The Garden is to engage all in the quest to know and to share the unconditional love of God."

Core Theology

Our core theology is evident in the vision of who we are. We say, "The Garden is a celebration of life, a journey into faith, and the soulful embrace of all." From this statement, we have been able to identify the core values that we try to uphold in our worship experience, in every team meeting, and wherever we go. Those core values are: spirituality, love, purposefulness, inclusiveness, creative excellence, celebration, and empowerment.

Because of our beliefs, our services are designed for celebration and inspiration; any teaching that occurs happens as a natural outcome of a celebrative, inspirational service. We want those who leave our services to know that life is good, to know that God is with them in their daily lives, and to be hopeful about what lies ahead. We do not consider worship a time for in-depth Bible study. We include biblical exegesis and interpretation only to the extent that it is pertinent for understanding a particular passage and its relationship to our everyday lives.

Relevancy is a key word for us. We want to be able to connect with persons wherever they are in life. The best thing any of us can hear after a Sunday service is, "Boy! How did you know what I am going through?" I feel that it is important to relate with people in a way that gives them hope in dealing with life's struggles and challenges. It's important that we lead them toward a place where they can experience for themselves the reality that God is with them and can guide their every action, word, and decision. We want to ignite the ember of faith within and do our part to nurture and encourage spiritual growth. Thus, we do not consider ourselves "churchy," but rather "spiritual" in trying to help people find their higher purpose and calling, and to help them live a life in tune with God's will and loving goodness.

We are very committed to inclusiveness as one of our core values, and we want everyone to feel welcomed, loved, and accepted without judgment. Everyone who walks through our doors (and actually those who don't, too!) is considered a child of God and an important member of God's family. We try to create a warm hospitable atmosphere and show honor and respect for the worth and dignity of every individual.

One way our society excludes, often unknowingly and unintentionally, is through language. We take great care to make all of our language inclusive. We are intentional about gender language as it relates to both humans and God. We use the word "partner," rather than "husband" or "wife," in order not to exclude our gay and lesbian brothers and sisters who are welcome at The Garden. Worship leaders use first-person pronouns, rather than second-person pronouns, as a way of underscoring our belief that there is no distinction between the leaders and the congregations. This also gives our worship a more conversational and less "preachy" tone.

I feel strongly that each of us in our respective congregations needs to be striving for creative excellence in everything we do. We push ourselves hard to do the very best we can each and every week and often find ourselves frustrated and perhaps ultracritical when we mess up a song or when the live transmission doesn't go flawlessly. The congregation is forgiving and laughs along with us when we make our mistakes, knowing full well that we are as human as they are and that things like that just happen. Our mistakes do create a bonding effect with those who come, even though we are constantly striving for excellence. Perhaps I should say that we are always working toward continual improvement and prefer not to repeat the same mistakes. We're very good, however, at making new ones! Each week, we just do the best we can and pray that God will continue to work in and through us to share the message we feel called to share.

The Planning Process

It is important to determine what working arrangement is best for you in your context. For us, the team concept was established early on as being basic to who we are, and so we began and continue with each worship service being developed by the Worship Design Team. This group meets each Tuesday from 6:00 to 8:00 P.M., and we plan the details for the upcoming services. Currently, we have all the details for the services prepared for the next two Sundays, and only if something unexpected occurs do we change the content of those services.

The procedure each week begins with checking in with each person, establishing those who have prayer needs, and opening with prayer. We then quickly verbally review the previous Sunday and explore any glitches that we need to correct. Then we look over the elements and flow we've established for the coming Sunday and make any necessary changes. For instance, this past week we had to make a change in a movie clip because the one we had hoped to use at the beginning of the service was not available. That happens rarely, but situations like that do arise, and we have to be prepared to accommodate them.

Next we look to the service to take place ten days hence. The sermon has been e-mailed to everyone several weeks in advance, and earlier conversations have yielded ideas for the various elements. We usually preview the video possibilities first, looking at movie clips and any "specials" we might produce or already have at our disposal. Once we determine the range of clips we have, we listen to the musical possibilities and try to determine which ones work best as set-up, which are best in the body of the service, and which are best for the "anchor" song. Since it is our goal to integrate the service as completely as possible, we make sure the music that is selected integrates with the point of the movie clips and is placed in the correct part of the order of the service.

Once the music and clips have been selected, we identify the participants and plan the flow. Often, we follow the lead of our creative director, who is a talented musician, actress, and director, and who has an excellent sense of how the mood and movement of the service should unfold. We discuss the bridging elements, the transitions from one segment to the next, the change of tone, and the elements that need to blend and support the theme of this Sunday's service. The order of service becomes what we refer to as the "flow," and it is e-mailed to all participants by Thursday morning and also sent to our administrative team leader who prepares the programs from the information we provide.

Timing

Timing is essential for our services because they take place within the confines of the eight or more theater performances that occur each week at Beef and Boards and the special brunches and receptions that occur on Sundays at Oak Hill. This planning requires close coordination with the live transmission between our two sites during our 10:15 services. Consequently, we create each service to last forty to forty-five minutes, and we use some regular time clusters for certain elements. For example, unless we have an unusual Sunday, the message is typically twelve minutes long and can be done either as one whole message, or divided into segments. The introduction/welcome is usually allocated two minutes, as is the prayer. The band sings three or four songs, and each one is approximately three to five minutes in length. The movie clips that we use are quite brief, usually no longer than two or three minutes, and our original videos are usually three to four minutes in length.

Music

Probably the most important element that distinguishes services at The Garden from services that are referred to as "contemporary" is the music we choose. As I mentioned above, it is our intent to create a well-integrated service, in which every part introduces, supports, or carries the theme. This is especially true when it comes to the music. There's usually a song that introduces the subject and either leads to the intro/welcome or follows it. That piece of music might ask a question about the morning's issue, or it might be a lighthearted song that just introduces the topic in a humorous way. One song, perhaps two, serve as transitional pieces between other elements of the service, and these songs reinforce the fabric of the message by weaving one image or thread of thought into another. A final song at the end is our "anchor" song—the one that "nails" the topic and pulls everything together.

It is impossible to overstate the importance of our music, and we are blessed to have wonderfully talented musicians who volunteer their time to rehearse each week and to spend their Sunday mornings sharing God's love through music. Music packs a powerful message and can act as a means to express emotion, to open hearts and minds and spirits, and to heal brokenness. The Garden staff has made some conscious decisions regarding the selection of the music we use in our services. As previously stated, we use inclusive language, avoiding gender-based references to God and to humanity. We use popular music that members of the congregation might have heard on a favorite (non-Christian) radio station during the week or on the way to The Garden. We use the sound of today's music, with electric guitar, bass, drum, and electronic keyboard; and all of our music supports the central theme of the day. Although each musical selection does not have to convey the entire message, each song is chosen to communicate a particular portion of the message and is placed at an appropriate spot in the service. We do not use traditional hymns, and most of the time our congregation does not participate by singing. There are occasions during which we encourage Gardeners to join us, and that typically meets with various degrees of success.

We made a conscious decision to use secular music as the bulk of our musical selections, although we do use some contemporary Christian songs. You will not hear repetitive praise choruses at The Garden, and that was the only adamant request I made at the outset. The primary reason is that I find the theology inadequate, and the language does not live up to our commitment to model inclusiveness.

The reason we have chosen to focus on secular pop music as a conduit to spirituality is because that is what our Gardeners usually listen to outside of church. We firmly believe that God speaks to us in all parts of life and that there is no separation between the sacred and the secular. It is exciting to discover that a song a Gardener may have heard numerous times takes on an entirely different meaning when it is heard in the context of a worship service.

Allow me to share a personal example to show what I mean. One Sunday three or four years ago, the topic was "Wrestling with Angels." The premise of the message was that our society's current love of angels was perhaps a statement about our desire for connection with a greater Force, or the "Holy," and that we were using angels as a substitute for God. The closing song was a song popular at the time, "I Am Your Angel." Our daughter, who had just graduated from college, was there that morning, and a week or two later, she said to me, "Mom, I can't hear that song now without thinking about The Garden." I tried to play it cool, but inwardly, my response was, "Yes! It works!" That's exactly what we want to have happen— our attendees realize the connection and know that God is within and around them at every moment. Music can make that happen.

As stated earlier, we make a point of using as much secular music as we possibly can, believing that, put in a new context, it can take on a very powerful meaning. If you visit The Garden, you will hear music performed by a band like that you might find at a rock concert or in a jazz bar. A small vocal ensemble, accompanied by electronic keyboard, guitar, bass, and percussion, provides music that is well known to the boomer generation. We like to take music that attendees might hear on any light rock or pop radio station, such as the music of Garth Brooks, Shania Twain, Elton John, Phil Collins, Eric Clapton, and others.

This intentional incorporation of the art, language, and idioms of popular culture serves to drive home the message each week in a very powerful way. Take, for instance, the Good Friday service we do each year, one that has become a "signature" service for us. As Gardeners enter, the sound track from *Schindler's List* is playing. Some of the music during the service that is interwoven with a clip from *Amistad* and narrative of the crucifixion story are songs such as "My One True Friend," "Tears in Heaven," "Streets of Philadelphia," and others of that genre. Using music that people are used to hearing on their car radios or on CD has a surprising effect when used to tell the story of our faith.

As mentioned previously, we avoid the use of "praise music" since its use would violate the heart of our core values. I have a personal bias against their repetitive choruses, the narrow confines of their theology, and the lack of inclusiveness in their lyrics. They fly in the face of several of our core values, and we will not violate those values. Thus, although we do sometimes use contemporary Christian music, like that of Sandi Patti, Susan Ashton, Amy Grant, Point of Grace, Michael W. Smith, or Stephen Curtis Chapman, we make sure the lyrics are appropriate to our values. I realize that not everyone shares the bias I have and may, in fact, find praise choruses meaningful. If it fits into your context, and you can use it without violating your integrity, then, of course, that would be your preference. Simply stated, praise music does not fit with what we are trying to do.

Bible Passage

We always refer to it as the "Bible passage" rather than "Scripture," again because we want to break down any barriers that are created by using terms that are unfamiliar to our attendees. Although I suspect there are traditional church members who believe that we should teach those who come the jargon of "real" church, I am not one of them. I fear that, for those unaccustomed to "church," our church language has served to separate us from God and one another, rather than to unite us and draw us closer to relationship with God.

We use various contemporary and modern language versions of the Bible passage in order to make certain the meaning and intent of the passage are understandable to the receivers. Our favorites include *The Message*, *The Promise*, *Today's English Version*, and *The New Living Translation*. We will use one translation and sometimes more than one, depending on how the message is best communicated.

Sometimes the passage and its background and context are explained during the message. Other Sundays, it might be read during an instrumental introduction to a song, while the words are displayed on screen. Sometimes we will create a skit, making an updated story of the Bible passage or use a contemporary rendering in juxtaposition with the Bible passage itself. We have created video pieces that convey the Bible passage or used a reader's theater type of approach. Our attempt is always to make sure people can understand what the passage is trying to say to us in today's world.

Video

Like many other church services, we use movie clips—today's art form—to introduce and drive home our subject and to illustrate the message. (We are very careful about obtaining the proper licenses and about honoring copyright rules and regulations.) We use multiple clips every Sunday, sometimes from several different movies, and sometimes using clips from the same movie throughout the service. We are very careful when it comes to language, violence, and sexual references; and we have begun printing a disclaimer in our weekly program, noting that our use of any particular clips does not necessarily mean that we endorse the film.

I'm not much of a movie buff, but fortunately, we have several people who are, and they have chosen to share their love of movies with us. One young woman, who came when we put out the first call to St. Luke's members to join us in this endeavor, not only loves movies, but also can remember virtually every scene in every movie. When we talk about a theme, a lightbulb goes off in her head, and she quickly jots down the name of a movie to revisit to see if it will work for us. There are others on our team who share the same kind of passion for movies, and they have added a whole new dimension and versatility to our services with their knowledge and expertise.

We are also fortunate to have gifted individuals on our video team who have the capacity to create and produce original videos to enhance our theme on any given Sunday. On some occasion, we use these videos to accompany a song the band is singing, and on other occasions, they are stand-alone pieces. We have sometimes narrated and visually illustrated a storybook to get a point across, and we have used original footage accompanied by a song such as "Angel" as our prodigal child Bible passage. A video called "The Amazing Maize Maze" was created when a team of folks headed to a cornfield in northern Indiana where a farmer had created a corn maze. The "Maize Maze" introduced the topic the Sunday we talked about being lost in life and unable to find our way.

One of our basic ingredients as a church is our worship, and yet I find that, far too often, little time is actually dedicated to understanding why we worship and allowing that to influence the way we worship. We're frequently content to do what's always been done and to follow the normal conventional church ways. Although that is still relevant for many, I fear the numbers are quickly dwindling; and if present trends continue, the church will be extinct and its guidance lost. We must be open to new ways of worshiping and new understandings of what worship is if we are going to reach new generations and far-reaching segments of our population. In my opinion, this is a life or death option; we must be willing to change if the church is to have any voice in the future.

Questions for Consideration

1. What are the core values of your congregation? Are you living true to them?

2. Identify your basic theology. How is that theology lived out in your worship services?
3. What new elements might you consider adding to your worship services that might reach new people?
4. What are the practices that you use to create your worship experiences? How might they be changed?
5. If you were going to choose music for a new service, where would you begin, and what type of music would you select?

CHAPTER 9

GETTING THE WORD OUT ABOUT THE GARDEN

Marketing to the Community

One of the key issues in starting a new ministry is getting the word out, and successful marketing in its various forms is the answer. When we first started The Garden, before it was called anything at all, I met with marketing professionals to gain their buy-in to the concept. They were the first persons with whom I met outside of the St. Luke's leadership, and their work laid the groundwork for all that has followed.

They named The Garden and developed the logo, which is still representative of who we are, but they did much more than that. They asked all the right questions, being certain to determine the part of the population we were trying to reach, and suggesting how we might best reach that segment. We were clear that we were trying to connect with unchurched boomers (the term we used at the beginning, but which we shy away from today), and our marketing efforts were targeted toward boomers.

In addition, our marketing aimed to help people realize that this was not the typical church. Our radio campaign used the phrase, "A church that's not even in a church." Although we had no intention of dissociating ourselves from The United Methodist Church, we also became aware that denominational affiliations were not necessarily appealing to today's generations and could even possibly be a deterrent.

To capture people's attention, a jingle was created. It was actually a remake of the hymn "The Gift of Love," but it was much more catchy. The initial campaign that our Marketing Team developed grew out of this thought: "Tired of four-letter words? Try these . . . hope, love, food, soul, song." Although we never used the "tired of four-letter word" part, that constituted the thought process behind the campaign. Thus, the newly created jingle became, "In The Garden, there's hope, food for the soul, helpful words to make your life whole." That jingle continues to be used today at the beginning of each service and in our radio spots.

The very first media blitz consisted of advertising on radio, TV, and in the newspaper. We chose the pop stations that had most of the listener audience that made up our target group and ran one-minute spots for three weeks prior to the launch of the first service. The TV spots were thirty-second clips that were fairly generic, with a flower opening and the same text that the radio spot had. Because we didn't have any actual footage of what The Garden was going to look like, we resorted to stock image but eventually replaced that with real footage showing the theater, the band, video screens, and casually dressed attendees.

Our newspaper ads did not run on the church page of Saturday's paper, but appeared on the movie page. Those we wanted to reach probably weren't perusing the church ads to see where they were going to go on Sunday morning, but instead were probably scanning the movies in town to see what they were going to do on Saturday night. Those ads were three-inch blocks, black on white, and white on black, with one of the four-letter words representing The Garden—HOPE, LOVE, SONG, FOOD, SOUL, and so on. These ads, too, appeared for a three-week period, but primarily on weekends and holidays.

I know many churches have had success with direct mail, but we elected not to use it in our area. Our research indicated that direct mail had only a 0.8 percent response ratio, and we didn't feel that the cost supported that small a return on investment. Instead, someone underwrote a four-color, multi-page brochure that was made available to St. Luke's members and constituents, and we asked them to hand them out to coworkers, neighbors, friends, or family who did not currently attend any church. We found this to be much less costly, and it turned out to be a positive tool for introducing The Garden to the community.

After the initial launch of The Garden, we shifted our approach a bit, using radio more in the summer, which is when people tend to listen more to the radio. We held our TV spots for winter when people stay indoors and often become couch potatoes. Later TV ads were on the cable channels and went on a "run-of-the-schedule" basis. This was fairly inexpensive and met with some success.

Our research shows that nearly two-thirds of Garden attendees during the first two years came to us as a result of the media marketing campaign. Slowly, that began to change as more and more people heard about us from others and showed up. Word of mouth is now our primary means of reaching people, although we are still intent on staying outwardly focused and continue to use media campaigns to reach new people.

During 2004, our media campaign consisted mainly of four flights on radio, one prior to Good Friday and Easter, one in the summer, one in the early fall, and one prior to Christmas Eve. We are currently on three radio stations, including one Latino station, and in the print media. Our tendency these days is to appear in the monthly or weekly publications rather than in the daily newspaper, and we tend to make sure we are in publications whose readership is in the African American community and in the gay and lesbian community. Needless to say, we also get free publicity from stories and press releases that capture people's attention.

This year, we also tried a card in a newcomer's packet. The recipient could redeem the card for a Good Earth Band CD when coming to The Garden at Beef and Boards or The Garden at Oak Hill for the first time. The Garden is also listed with the St. Luke's ad in the Saturday newspaper and in the yellow pages. I'm not sure how effective these are, but they still get our name before the public.

In about the second year of our existence, we made a thirty-minute infomercial about The Garden that ran on a station owned by a St. Luke's member and on cable channels. It was a costly undertaking, but we still use it on occasion to give a flavor of what The

Garden is like at conferences and workshops. I'm not sure I would recommend expending the time and energy to create such a massive endeavor.

At one point in time, that same St. Luke's member ran copies of our services on his station. Each service had to be edited to a thirty-minute program, and we inserted parts of prior TV ads and part of the infomercial as segue from one section of the service to another. Obviously, the TV version could not include any of the movie clips, since we are not licensed to show them other than to our attendees, and that was why we had to replace them with original footage.

One piece of marketing that we still make available is a postcard that we have on the information tables. The card is for Gardeners to take and send to friends who might be interested in knowing about The Garden. It says simply, "Having a wonderful time here at The Garden. Hope you can join us some Sunday at 8:15, 9:15, or 10:15 at Beef and Boards, and 10:15 at Oak Hill," with the addresses included. These appear to be quite popular, and we've had a good response.

I hope it goes without saying that marketing must include the basic ingredients of signage that I've talked about earlier. At both sites, we have crafted professional signage that covers the billboards and marquees of the business in which we're housed on Sunday mornings and advertises the presence of The Garden and the times of services. Directional signs are also important to remember. In addition, at the time of our second launch, St. Luke's put up two three-foot high by nine-foot long banners at the front of the church. Thousands of cars pass by each day, and St. Luke's members see them each Sunday and are reminded of The Garden so they can tell others. Let me say that it's important to have signage that is of good quality and highly visible. A little real estate sign outside the site of worship will hardly do the trick.

All in all, I would have to say that a good marketing plan is essential for a successful start of a new ministry. In order for it to be effective, however, it is imperative to be clear on the image we want to convey and know for certain to whom we want to communicate our image and message. It's important for congregations to consider marketing dollars as one element of a start-up budget.

Communication within The Garden

As The Garden grew and flourished, it became necessary to develop a way to communicate important information internally. We were blessed when a retired professor of journalism appeared on our doorstep and offered her services, embellished with her intense desire to help Gardeners connect with one another. Little did we know what an impact she was to make on the life of The Garden, and little were we able to absorb the impact created by her sudden death in mid-April of 2004. We are still reeling from the loss.

When she came forward, our communication consisted almost entirely of basic announcements on screen each Sunday and in the Sunday program. If we needed to communicate other information, we sent out postcards or phoned team members. With the arrival of an expert in the field, we began to enlarge our efforts, starting first with a quarterly newsletter. This publication consists of a page one letter and comments from the pastor, profiles of band and/or other team members, a spiritual journey, and a centerfold that focuses on an issue or activity that The Garden has undertaken.

A year or so after the inception of the quarterly *Garden News*, we added a monthly two-page publication called "What's Up in The Garden?" This piece appears on the tables and at the information tables on the first Sunday of the month, and it includes the birthdays during the upcoming month, the themes and titles for each Sunday, and a "in our thoughts and prayers" section that lists those who have requested prayers or are recovering from illnesses or surgeries or are grieving. It usually has an article about an event that has just happened or one that is about to happen, such as a picture and article of the recent women's retreat, or a picture of the people who brought toys for the children in the hospital ward in Eldoret, Kenya.

In 2002, we began a new offering, once again with the initiative of our fearless and talented communication team founder and leader. This time it was The Garden *Enews*. This is e-mailed to some eight hundred recipients each Wednesday and contains a synopsis of the last Sunday service and a preview of what's coming the next week. It, too, includes prayer requests and concerns and often interviews with Gardeners about one of the upcoming topics, getting their responses and ideas. This has proved to be a popular addition to our communication efforts and has been well received.

Our Communication Team, like our Marketing Team, is filled with those who have expertise in their respective areas; and their work has been invaluable. Willing workers have learned under this skilled professional, and our publications and marketing efforts show a quality that is hard to beat. Again, the persons who have responded to the ministry of The Garden and offered their skills and gifts have become our greatest asset. We couldn't function without them in any areas of The Garden's life, and that is true when it comes to our communication and marketing needs.

www.the-garden.org

We are only beginning to explore the reach of our Web page, and we are probably behind the times in those efforts. Currently, all our publications are accessible online, and the written sermons are archived there. Basic information about our Garden sites can be found on our Web page, and we are looking at how to enhance our ministry through the use of the Internet.

Our plans include live streaming of our services, probably in the fall of 2004, and establishing online study groups, book groups, and "discussion" chat rooms focusing on the various topics we explore each week. Our strategy plan includes investigating what it looks like to become a "Virtual Garden." Although we aren't where we'd like to be yet, I'm convinced that this is the future of ministry. We must all find ways to reach more and more people, and the Internet is an excellent tool for doing that.

We at The Garden are committed to being one of the voices for what Marcus Borg, in his book *The Heart of Christianity*, refers to as the "emerging way of being Christian." There is uniqueness in The Garden because of our openness, our spiritual nature, and our unconventional and nontraditional outreach. These are undergirded by our progressive theology, and I want very much for a different voice to be heard in the milieu of contemporary life. The Internet may be one of the ways that can happen.

Questions for Consideration

1. What marketing plan are you considering for getting the word out about your ministry?
2. What resources do you have to help with external marketing and internal communication?
3. How would you rate your internal communication? What could improve it?
4. How are you using the Internet to share the faith message?

CHAPTER 10

IT TAKES LOVE TO MAKE
A GARDEN GROW

Each week, it takes hundreds of hours and megatons of energy to make The Garden happen. I'd like to walk you through a typical week of preparation for Sunday morning and highlight some of the teams that work outside the parameters of the worship experience. The commitment level is substantial since the work it takes to create a Sunday service requires more than one hour on a Sunday morning. First, let's look at the teams that do the work to ensure that Sunday mornings happen. I've already talked a bit about the worship team and how its Tuesday evening meetings evolve, but there is work that must take place both prior to that meeting and in the days that follow.

Message Team

The Message Team is the group that starts the ball rolling for our Sunday services. This team meets approximately once a quarter and sets the themes and titles for the services four to six months in advance. Even though it's sometimes necessary to change the theme or the order of the work the Message Team does, we try out best to honor the work that that team has done and adhere to their proposals for Sunday themes. Most team members come to the quarterly gathering well prepared, with ideas that others have shared with them or with themes that have arisen because they were inspired by a piece of music or a clip from a movie. The majority of the themes that are proposed represent the felt needs of our congregation, and of the larger Indianapolis community. It is important to have a sense of the needs around us, and to respond to those in the best way that we can.

Once the themes for the upcoming months are established, that information is e-mailed to our administrative team leader, who creates two worksheets for the worship design team members. One is a composite listing of the themes and titles that lie ahead, and the other is an individual worksheet for each Sunday theme. On that worksheet spaces are left for that team's brainstorming of video and music ideas, as well as a place to note any "specials," such as handouts, special videos, drama skits or character sketches, and so forth. There's a space for the Bible passage that I select as I begin work on each service and a space for the prayer team to share its input. On the back side of the worksheet is space for us to jot down the "flow" as it evolves in the course of the worship design team meeting.

Music Teams

Our two bands, each composed at any one time of eight to fourteen instrumentalists and vocalists, rehearse for three hours each week. The Good Earth Band at Beef and Boards rehearses each Monday evening, and the Oak Hill band rehearses on Wednesday evenings. For the most part, the members work out the harmonies and create their own arrangements as they rehearse. We are blessed to have extremely talented musicians at both sites, and all the band members are committed to giving their best each week.

To make sure the possible music selections are narrowed down to a manageable number, the two band directors get together each week prior to our Worship Design Team meeting. They meet to discuss the possibilities for the service that we will concentrate on that evening, typically the service that is one and one-half weeks away. The music for the upcoming Sunday has already been set, and the Good Earth Band will have already rehearsed it. Because of the live transmission between our two sites, the two directors will coordinate arrangements of the music to assist in the critical nature of timing.

Video Team

Just as the music teams must do additional work, not only at rehearsal, but also on their own, so, too, does the video team. The members of this team have already heard some of the brainstorming ideas from the rest of the worship design team, but it becomes their responsibility to find those movie clips and others and to bring them (cued) to the worship design team for viewing. After the decisions are made regarding which clips we will use, the video team makes certain that those clips are in the right order and ready to go when Sunday morning rolls around. This is the team that also prepares any original video work that we have chosen to show on a particular Sunday, and this team shoots and edits our 10% Charitable Contributions video for each month's recipient.

Tech Team

Another team on whom we rely heavily is our Tech Team. Although we functioned for nearly eight years with an all-volunteer tech team, our desire to "take it to the next level" in terms of excellence meant that we needed to consider hiring someone to prepare the slides each week. In 2003, we began paying someone to prepare the slides for each Sunday, and that has definitely improved the quality of our Sunday work.

Remember that we are intentional about providing as much visual reinforcement to our Sunday theme as possible, and that means that we put everything we can on screen. A typical slide show on Sundays, including the pre-service announcements, consists of approximately two hundred slides. The backgrounds are all selected to coordinate with the theme, the quote being cited, or the lyrics of the song being sung. The slides with the announcements are created to attract Gardeners' attention and serve to remind them of upcoming events and other specific details.

At each site, we have professional sound and light technicians who are paid part-time staff. This began with Beef and Boards, where the theater's stage manager came aboard at the very beginning. I suspect it was largely to protect his sound and light board from volunteers messing up all the settings for the current theater production. Nonetheless, he has become very committed to what we do each week, and he works very hard setting the light cues that match the tone of the music and the message we are hoping to convey. Even though the lighting is subtle, it has a profound effect on the congregation.

As I mentioned earlier, we do not have the same setup at our second site, but we felt it was necessary to hire a professional to run the sound board, especially because it is owned by the proprietors of the banquet hall. It has to be in good working order for both them and us, and we believe that a professional does that best.

The rest of the Tech Team is made up of volunteers. These are the people who run the slides each week, cue and run the video clips, coordinate any quotes and visuals in the sermon with the preacher, as well as coordinate the timing efforts between the two sites at our 10:15 services to facilitate the live transmission. Volunteers operate the camera each week for that transmission, and this team communicates on site with radios and between sites with cell phones. These are busy people on Sunday mornings!

During our third service at Beef and Boards (and currently the only service at Oak Hill), the tech folks have to coordinate everything for their site and closely monitor the progress of the other site to make sure we're going to be ready for the transmission at the same time. Recently, we have begun using "meditative slides" accompanied by our keyboardists to make any time lag between the two sites less noticeable. (Typically it is as little as a few seconds, but on occasion, it has been as long as a minute.) That means that our keyboardists are also a part of the radio network at their respective sites so that they can help smooth the transitional points. The members of the Tech Team are constantly working to make what we do as good as it can be, and we have recently installed new equipment at the theater, replacing our seven-year-old projectors, motorizing the screens, moving the tech booth upstairs separate from the sound booth, adding new monitors, and upgrading to DVD technology. The Tech Team's work is excellent, and the end product shows it.

Prayer Team

The Prayer Team also has direct effect on each Sunday's service. There are team leaders at each site, and they counsel and train team members in the nature of our prayer time. They rotate leading prayer each week and usually participate in the Worship Design Team in order to be aware of where the prayer comes in the flow and what elements it connects. Again, the one who is praying tries to tie the prayer to the central theme of the day and, of course, is sure to reflect the corporate needs of our faith community.

Loading Team

Each Sunday morning begins with the work of the Loading Team. Originally, the team was five or six people strong and loaded amplifiers, keyboards, hospitality needs, programs, and more into a couple of vans for transport to the theater. Because each site now offers storage space, the team is composed of only two or three persons, and except on special occasions such as Easter, their load is not massive. This team is basic, however, to our operation because it is the team that arrives at the theater and banquet hall with the essential items needed for our other teams to begin work. Typically, the Beef and Boards Loading Team arrives at St. Luke's at 6:30 A.M. and is unloading at the theater by 7:00. The team for Oak Hill can work a bit later in the morning since there is only a 10:15 service at that location.

Hospitality Teams

I've already mentioned the work of our many Hospitality Team members. Suffice it to say that they are the heart of The Garden, and it is their role to be that warm, friendly presence that greets our Gardeners as they come and leave. They are "in the loop" for Sunday preparation by being informed of any handouts that are being used during or at the end of the service, as well as by knowing the details for communion, baptism, Christmas Eve, Good Friday, or other special occasions.

Speaking of handouts, it is important to share more about that item, the role of those who prepare or purchase them, and the role of the hospitality folk who hand them out. When it fits, we offer attendees something to take home with them to reinforce what we've talked about that Sunday. One Sunday, when we talked about "letting go," we gave everyone a cling-free sheet that many of us use in our dryers. We've handed out footballs with the Bible passage or pom-poms on Super Bowl Sunday. Attendees have received purchased compasses on the Sunday we talked about looking for direction in our lives. We've created business cards for everyone to take, identifying each one as a child of God; we passed out items for them to put in their paper bag for their survival kit for life. The Hospitality Team is almost always involved in the distribution of those items, as well as the saplings or seed packets on Easter, the nails on Good Friday, and the candles on Christmas Eve.

Sometimes we hand out cards or other items that a band member, who is also a very talented artist, has created. When we recently talked about our strengths, we referred to the movie *Brother Bear* and gave each person a totem (a God-given gift) that our artist-in-residence made. This is the person who coordinates our art fair, which has become a regular summer event, climaxing our once-a-year Sunday theme of creativity. Again, this person is a volunteer who has offered to share her talents with the entire Garden family.

Let's go back to a conversation about the teams that work throughout the week in order to make The Garden what it is. I've mentioned previously the work of the Marketing Team and Communication Team, as well as our bands and music teams and the others directly related to worship. Now I'd like to highlight the hard work of those who function behind the scenes.

Leadership Team

The Leadership Team is really the visioning body of The Garden, is composed of representatives from both sites, and it meets every other month. The team is currently exploring two major issues. One is the recent commitment for us to be intentional, but selective, about multi-site ministry. Numerous opportunities to go into other locales are being presented to us, and it's important for us to sort through the possibilities and assess those with the greatest potential to reach those whom we want to reach, including new age groups and new demographic groups.

The other major decision has to do with succession. The unexpected death of our communication team leader has shaken us all, and we realize that if any one of a dozen or more key leaders suffered a heart attack or was hit by a truck today, we are totally unprepared. There's no one standing beside us or behind us who understands the whole picture, and could take the reigns. Certainly, there are many who know parts of what is needed, but we have not done a good job in keeping prospective replacements fully informed and in tune with what is happening.

In addition, a plan for my succession that fits within our denominational restraints must be shaped. Our conference will receive a new bishop during 2004, and our district superintendent (personnel officer) will be retiring in 2005. The retiring bishop and current district superintendent have been supportive of both St. Luke's and The Garden, but there isn't a guarantee that that support will continue in the same manner. It's important that we map out several possible scenarios and communicate those to the St. Luke's leadership, who speaks on our behalf on such issues.

Creative Team

Another team that was formed this past year is the Creative Team. It is this team's objective to come up with ideas that can supplement worship or make The Garden more creative in a variety of ways. Most of the ideas generated so far have related to worship, which has been good primarily because the Worship Design Team is so task-oriented when we get together each week that we aren't as creative as we could be. This team also began putting together a directory of Gardeners, with pictures, and has conducted an online survey to garner more information that can shape the direction of The Garden and of the team's creative efforts.

Comfort and Care Team

How do we care for Gardeners? It is through our Comfort and Care Team. Each site has a leader who monitors the "comfort and care line" (a telephone messaging system) that we set up a few years ago. Gardeners are urged to call the care line with their own needs or those of other Gardeners. Comfort and Care Team members follow up on a need that comes to their attention with a phone call or visit. This really is the pastoral care arm of our ministry. Several of our Comfort and Care Team members are trained as Stephen Ministers, and they are well prepared to make hospital calls and to make contacts in the case of bereavement. In addition, the part-time clergy person (an ordained Disciples of Christ minister) is our key pastoral care contact person. She works with the team's members to coordinate our caring efforts. Incidentally, to make sure Gardeners know about the team and its work, we periodically give them refrigerator magnets with the comfort and care line phone number on them.

Development Team

A team that has one of the biggest challenges is The Garden's Development Team. This is the team that oversees the financial matters of The Garden, helps prepare the budget, writes grants to solicit financial support from foundations, and tries to raise our congregation's awareness of the connection between our faith and the use of our financial resources.

This team typically meets on a monthly basis and keeps tabs on the income and expenses. Various team members oversee the administration of the grants we have received, while others take an active role in setting our budget. Currently, the team is sending out a letter asking Gardeners to provide funds to match a grant that we have secured to create a music database by theme. Although the sum needed is already provided for in our budget, the receipt of additional funds designated for that purpose would relieve the budget of the necessity of providing those monies out of Sunday offerings.

In addition, the Development Team is constantly exploring new and creative ways to fund The Garden. It has also taken the lead in facilitating conversations with possible funding entities in our community. Although the task is difficult, the team leader and all the team members operate with great faithfulness and with sincere dedication to the well-being of The Garden. This team has been a godsend for me, making it possible to share the responsibility of the financial matters of our ministry.

Garden Youth Group and The Garden Kids

Two newly formed teams work with our children and youth. Prior to a couple of years ago, we did not have a Garden Youth Group, but someone with young teens changed that. The GYG, as it is called, has become outreach-oriented, being involved in helping ministries that improve the lives of other youth in our community. They don't meet every week but work together to assist others on an as-needed basis.

Our newest team is The Garden Kids Team. This is composed of eight to ten parents of children ages two through twelve, and they work regularly to create curriculum that is "Garden-esque." That means that representatives meet weekly with the Worship Design Team in order to be clear on the focus on upcoming Sundays, and then they create activities and materials that coordinate with the theme the rest of their family is experiencing.

Although many of our parents prefer to have their children remain with them at their table, others have responded well to The Garden Kids Program. To assist all families, The Garden Kids Team has created a regular item for Gardeners to take with them each week. It is "The Garden-to-Go," and it is found on the back of the quotation sheet that is prepared for Gardeners each week. It summarizes the main points of the morning, includes the Bible passage in a children's version, and offers some conversation starters for families to use, whether or not they participate in the Kids Group. This new ministry just officially began on Easter of 2004, and it is meeting with wonderful success!

Charitable Contributions Team and Outreach Team

Because we are intent on being outwardly focused, two teams are extremely important for us—our 10% Charitable Contributions Team and our Outreach Team. These are the two teams that make certain our efforts are spent trying to help others in our community and around the world. The 10% Charitable Contributions Team solicits suggestions for possible recipients from Gardeners twice a year. They then begin to sort through the groups that are suggested, test them against the guidelines they have set up, and create a calendar of the recipients for the coming year. Once an organization is selected, that information is passed on to the Worship Design Team for putting on the calendar. An announcement is on screen and in the program every Sunday telling Gardeners the name of the month's recipient that will receive 10 percent of the money they put in our watering cans in the course of that month.

A designated team member is responsible for greeting the representatives from the organization when they come to The Garden to receive their check and the video that has been created for them. The group also tries to raise the awareness of our Gardeners and urges them to volunteer their time and talent if a particular organization snags their attention.

The Outreach Team has undertaken a number of endeavors to keep The Garden connected with our community. It has coordinated efforts to write notes and cards to send to local retirement communities and has urged participation in Habitat projects and other work projects. Currently, its major task is coordinating an effort to fight the HIV/AIDS epidemic in Africa. To that end, The Garden is collaborating with the Indiana University School of Medicine–Kenya program. I will describe this undertaking more in chapter 13, but I can tell you that dreaming big is producing some remarkable results.

Lead Team

One last team that I'll mention is our Lead Team. This team consists of the pastor and creative director, who are the key leaders at the dinner theater, and the two anchors and the music director from our second site. We meet every Friday from 11:00 A.M. until 2:00 P.M., have lunch, and process all that is happening around us. It is our attempt to be on the same page and to build mutually satisfying relationships with one another as we live out our ministry. There are times that we just catch up with one another, and there are times when we have to prepare for upcoming events. At other times, there are pressing issues that demand our attention, but our desire is to find the best possible answer to whatever situation we may be facing, and to do it together as a team.

It takes lots of time, energy, and commitment to make a ministry like The Garden successful. Together, our teams spend several hundred hours each week tending to the ministry of The Garden. The dedication has been immense, and I believe that each team member truly feels that he or she is living out God's call on his or her life through the ministry each has chosen at The Garden. We are blessed to have such wonderful people call The Garden their spiritual home.

We were recently asked to describe our model for leadership development, and to do it visually. We wound up illustrating a seed that takes root, grows and blossoms, and then creates more seedlings that take root and blossom and bloom. The point of our drawing was to say that we don't have a systematic way to train and equip our leaders. Rather, they seem to emerge naturally, in what we call an "organic" fashion. We are able to plant seeds of God's love that grab hold of hearts and spirits, change lives, and move people to give of themselves to others. We want to be there to help identify the new sprouts, nurture the growth, and watch them bloom.

Questions for Consideration

1. What working groups do you believe to be necessary to make a new ministry function well?
2. What is the leadership style that will work best in your setting?
3. What is your method for developing new leaders in your congregation?

CHAPTER 11

MONEY AND THE GARDEN

As I mentioned earlier in this book, financing a ministry such
as The Garden is tricky business. We know that one major
turnoff when it comes to church is the complaint, "All they
ever talk about is money." We were determined not to be guilty of
that no-no. Yet there is an inextricable link between our growth in
faith and the way we use our financial gifts and resources, and
therein lies our dilemma. Obviously, it takes money to operate any
endeavor, and that is true of The Garden, too. What are we to do?

At the start, we were intentional about not asking for money during the service, and we have maintained that stance since the
beginning. Part of our early learning was that, with the open nature
of our theology, offering people a formula for faith that included
telling them to tithe was not a part of our DNA. We talked to many
who had worked with those coming new to the faith and determined that we should not expect the ministry to be totally under-
written by those who attend. Although the donations from
Gardeners continue to grow, they do not cover all the expenses for
such a creative undertaking.

That is one of the reasons for staying connected to the larger
local church. St. Luke's provides office space for The Garden, and
it currently provides the pastoral support items of our budget. That
includes salary, benefits, and expense account. Because we're under
the wing of the home church, St. Luke's, our attendance is counted
into their total for each Sunday and is included, therefore, in the
calculations for the apportionments paid to our Annual

Conference. In 2004, St. Luke's will be paying nearly $500,000 to the South Indiana Conference, by far the largest of any church. Because The Garden is not an officially recognized church, but rather falls in the satellite category, we do not pay a separate amount of apportionments. That, too, is an advantage and allows us to use our resources for ministry.

The fact that we do not own a facility also helps in the expense portion of The Garden's budget. That means that the funds we raise are not used for bricks and mortar or for the maintenance of a monstrous building. We have only to install, update, and maintain the equipment in each of our sites; that is really our only capital expense. As I have said, the space at Beef and Boards has been donated since the very beginning; and after 2004, the space at the banquet hall will also be donated, eliminating the need for rent in our budget. Thus, our Garden budget is as scaled down and geared toward ministry as we believe it can be.

It might be helpful if I outlined what our 2004 budget (for the two sites, minus clergy compensation, which is paid by St. Luke's) looks like. Out of a total budget of $524,368, we pay the following expenses:

Personnel	$243,503	46% of budget
Rent	$ 63,000	12% of budget
Tech equipment	$ 20,000	4% of budget
Marketing	$ 35,000	7% of budget
Administration	$ 27,450	5% of budget
Training	$ 10,000	2% of budget
Grant Match	$ 18,700	4% of budget
Hospitality	$ 32,000	6% of budget
Programming costs	$ 28,100	5% of budget
Charitable Contribution*	$ 29,325	8% of budget
Miscellaneous	$ 4,500	1% of budget

*This sum represents 8% of total budget and 10% of Sunday offering receipts.

A look at our sources of income yields the following results:

Sunday Offerings	$293,248	56% of budget
Hospitality	$ 17,592	3% of budget

| Conference Grant | $100,000 | 19% of budget |
| Miscellaneous* | $113,520 | 22% of budget |

*This sum is gathered from special drives, a few pledges to The Garden, the marketing of some Garden products, some programming fees, and various special gifts.

It is probably important to note that it is our intent every year to overbudget for our expenses and underbudget our income. At year-end, when a large portion of our revenue comes in, we have managed to come out even.

Because we have not expected our congregation to underwrite our ministry totally, we have had to be creative about seeking other sources of funding. Although this is unique to this type of ministry, I have a concern that this same situation may soon be true for even our traditional churches. I recently spent four Mondays in a civic conversation on the topic of faith and money, and statistics tell us that mainline denominations are in for some rough sailing in the days ahead. Only some of our more evangelical brothers and sisters come close to having their members tithe 10 percent, and even where that is the expectation, the percentage is more likely to be in the 7 to 8 percent range. Most mainline denominations report that giving probably averages in the 1 to 2 percent range, and it is decreasing.

I see this trend as a crisis in our faith. If we as the church are really fulfilling our mission and helping people have an encounter with the loving God, the one who transforms our lives, then having enough money will not be an issue. I fear, however, that we have become too irrelevant to today's society and have lost any voice of influence we once had. We focus on nonessential issues, giving out a judgmental, unaccepting message, and wonder why the traditional church is dying. I firmly believe that if we can help people understand how much God loves them and that God's love is overabundant, lives will be changed and our world will be totally different. When something positive and meaningful happens in someone's life, it is a natural tendency to want to share that and give back. There is more than enough to go around and plenty more to share.

This has been a hard lesson for me to absorb. When our Leadership Team reached a consensus about giving 10 percent of our

Sunday offerings to a different charitable organization each month, I have to admit that I cringed. How would we make it at the end of the year? Our agreement with St. Luke's is that we will be "budget neutral" to the St. Luke's budget. That means that we don't cost anything other than the pastoral support items that St. Luke's has agreed to pay.

I was frightened by our consensual decision and wondered what would happen. And yet, I'm happy to report that we have enough—more than enough really—and we have always been able to honor the commitment to St. Luke's that we made at the outset. In addition, we have been able to model, in a subtle way, what we profess to believe. We are to share what we have with others; that's how we can influence our world.

Whenever I opt for abundance in lieu of scarcity, I remember the story told in all four Gospels of Jesus feeding the five thousand (Matthew14:13-21, Mark 6:30-44, Luke 9:10-17, John 6:1-14). I'm certain you remember what it is, but a few years ago, as I was studying the Luke passage in preparation for preaching, I received an entirely new understanding of what happened in that story.

Today's English Version tells us that it was nearing the end of a long day, and the disciples came to Jesus and said to him, "Send the people away so that they can go to the villages and farms around here and find food and lodging, because this is a lonely place." Jesus responded to them by saying, "You yourselves give them something to eat." Jesus' friends seemed to be a bit taken aback, and said, "All we have are five loaves and two fish," and there were approximately five thousand people gathered there at the time.

Then Jesus instructed his disciples to have the people all sit down in groups of fifty or so each, which they did. Then Jesus took the bread and fish, thanked God, broke them, and gave them to the disciples to hand out. The remarkable part of the story is the conclusion: "They all ate and had enough, and the disciples took up twelve baskets of what was left over."

Now the Bible doesn't exactly put it this way, but this is how I suspect the scene unfolded. I doubt seriously that those who came to hear Jesus would have come empty-handed. Journeys could be long, and the way could be hard. My guess is that they had a sandwich, some bread, a little wine, and some other goodies in the knapsacks.

When they saw that Jesus was willing to trust God, and share his meager amount of food with them, they were moved to do the same. Slowly, bags of food began emerging from satchels and bags, and sandwiches were broken in two, or in three or four pieces, and everyone started passing what they had brought around, and sharing it with the others in their group. The miracle, to my mind, is not that Jesus performed some supernatural miracle that day. Rather, the miracle is that he trusted God enough to share what he had and not try to hoard it for himself. His example inspired others, and they followed suit. The fact that they all began to share was the miracle; and in the end, there was "more than enough."

There's one more thing that should go without saying. We must be good, responsible stewards of the resources we have been given. I think that means we provide ample information on the funds received and show how they are used. This is an issue of integrity and trust, and we must be faithful to the trust that our congregation places in us as their spiritual leader. I doubt that any of us are extravagant and splurge recklessly, but we have to keep faith with the covenant we make about the use of our time, talent, and treasure. Good stewardship is a must.

That summarizes my theology of giving, but let me say that I find it hard sometimes to step out in faith, trusting that there will be enough. Even when the past proves that there is abundance and not scarcity, I often find myself faltering and second-guessing myself and others, instead of steadfastly holding to that trust in God. I wonder when I'll learn.

Having said that, I have to confess that I'm facing a Sunday in the near future when our theme is "Money Talk." It will focus around the faithful use of the money and other financial resources God has given us; and it will also announce to The Garden the beginning of a Garden endowment, or more aptly, a Garden "non-building" fund. It is our intent to build an endowment so that we can continue to be faithful to the ministry to which we are called and guarantee the long-term financial stability of The Garden. We've discovered that people do, indeed, give generously, but sometimes it takes longer than expected to lead people to understanding the positive power the fruitful use of their financial resources can have in our world through the church.

In the meantime, we continue to explore other avenues to raise funds for the ministry of The Garden. We have received start-up support for our second site from our Annual Conference (our denominational body of which every clergy in southern Indiana is a member)—a three-year grant in the amount of $250,000. That has helped cover the first two years' rent and purchase the equipment we need, while also helping provide compensation for our paid staff. Since we rely heavily on volunteers, that grant, along with Sunday contributions, is underwriting the cost of the new venue.

We have also sought and received a grant to enable us to develop a database of the music resources we have used over the past nine years and tie it to the themes of the various services. We continue to pursue the possibility of grants from family foundations and other groups that fund faith-based organizations. Our attempts have met with mixed success, and church-related bodies tend to be our best candidates for funding. Nonetheless, we are building relationships and applying for funds from groups that have a vested interest in a designated area of ministry. For instance, the Garden Youth Group recently received a $1500 grant from the Indianapolis Colts to purchase books for the children who are involved in one of the GYG mission projects. Other such possibilities exist in our community and yours, and we all need to be aware and apply for any and all that might fit.

Another part of our strategy plan includes a source of income we call "Exportable/Transportable Products." That means that one of our goals is to become a resource for other churches who are interested in developing this kind of ministry. Some of that might be in the area of coaching and training, and another part might be the products themselves. The production of our music database is the first step in that process. It is our hope to be able to make available on the Internet listings of the songs, the videos, the scripture, the theme, the title, and even the sermons that related to any theme or topic we've discussed over the past eight years. We have a wealth of material collected in thousands of hours of study and research that could ease the process of preparing services such as ours for other churches. I know this would have been a huge help for us, had anyone been doing the kind of thing we were doing. We know others are interested, and we want to help and help our coffers at the same time.

"Creative Partnerships" is also a part of our strategy plan. It feeds into our fund-raising efforts, as it provides resources as "gifts-in-kind" and alleviates the need for purchasing or leasing the goods or services. The partnerships with the owners of our two sites are examples of what I'm talking about, as is our win-win arrangement with St. Luke's.

Another example might be the cooperative working relationship we have with our video production resources. We pay our video photographer a retainer fee and ask him to produce original videos for us, and to prepare our 10% Charitable Contribution video each month. He is a professional, and he works for a video production company. His camera is a $60,000 item, and he has an edit suite for the final preparation of his video creations. His agreement with his employer is that he can use both the camera and the editing equipment for Garden productions, as well, and that allows us to have topnotch video capabilities. Even though this is an unofficial partnership, it is one that has worked well for all parties involved.

One last partnership that I will mention is with the finance office at St. Luke's. We keep our own records and count our Sunday offerings ourselves. However, the St. Luke's accountant prepares and holds all of our official financial records. They give us a listing of donors and present us with monthly statements of our Garden accounts, which, combined with the records we keep, give us a good handle on our financial status at any given moment. Unlike some of the people who work in finance, those who work at St. Luke's are pleasant and go far beyond the course of duty to help us and make things easier and more complete for The Garden. We are grateful to them for their cooperative spirit and excellent work.

Needless to say, all of our churches need to have funds to live out our ministries, and those funds seem increasingly difficult to come by. However, I believe that, if we focus on sharing the message we are called to share, if we trust God, if we model our belief in abundance, and if we help people grow in their faith, the needed monies will come.

Questions for Consideration

1. How would you articulate your theology of money? What are the ties between faith and money for you?
2. What are your church's financial needs? How would you rate your quality of stewardship of the resources you've been given?
3. What creative sources of revenue might be available to your congregation?
4. What are the essential elements for ministry that must be funded?

CHAPTER 12

GETTING OUR HANDS DIRTY

In this chapter, I will outline the work I do as the primary preacher for The Garden, and as its lead pastor. In a nutshell, I see my role as consisting of three essential ingredients: preaching, visioning, and empowering. I will attempt to describe what I mean by those three and how I try to live them out on a daily basis.

Allow me to share first my philosophy of worship and preaching. Our intent for worship is to inspire those who attend and give each person a sense of hope that he or she is not alone and that "I can make it through the week." We state that our goal for worship is celebration and inspiration. We want people to feel that life is good, that their lives are worthwhile, and to experience that sense of inspiration that I've mentioned. Our hope is that we have, in one way or another, engaged their hearts in such a way that their relationship with God is closer and deeper than when they arrived.

To meet that goal, we work very hard to make our worship services an integrated whole. Although it would probably be much simpler to create each part of the service independently from every other part of the service, that can wind up feeling unfocused and disjointed. I hope that no one will leave The Garden and wonder what point we were trying to get across that day. It is carried and advanced by every element of the service. Every song, every video clip, the words of the prayer, the introduction and welcome, and the message are all tied together to create the message. Because of that thrust, it is not my responsibility to carry the weight of the entire message on my shoulders. It is a shared mission for all of us who create and participate in each Sunday's worship experience.

From my perspective, there are several key ingredients for conveying the spoken message effectively and persuasively. My guess is that there are many who would not agree with me, but through the years, the ones I'm about to share have been authenticated time and time again.

One key element for me is relevancy. Someone has called this "where the message meets the pavement." In other words, does the message we are sharing have anything at all to do with the daily lives of the receivers? If it is totally unrelated to the normal struggles and ups and downs of life, I would suggest that we are being irrelevant at best, downright boring at worst. We must be able to identify with the felt needs of our congregations in order to connect with them and have a small influence on the direction of their lives in the next hours, days, weeks, or years.

Another important key for good preaching, in my view, is to be real. When it comes to the person who is speaking, that equates to being honest about what we believe and being willing to be vulnerable about our own human frailties. I'm aware that there are some clergypersons who prefer to remain aloof and distant from the members of their congregations, but I feel that it is important for us to share our questions, our doubts, our struggles, as well as the challenges we face. I have a personal bias against making myself the hero of any story, but I have no problem laughing at myself and at my foibles and foolish mistakes. That is one of the ways in which I try my best to be human and real and authentic.

I think that carries over to everyone who is part of The Garden. One of the charges that is sometimes leveled at traditional church folks is that they are hypocritical. They look good on Sunday mornings, but their behavior the rest of the week is not necessarily in tune with their superficial Sunday piety. My experience has been that, no matter how "together" someone may appear, each one of us struggles in some significant ways. There is no perfect family; there is no perfect relationship; there are no perfect children. Our willingness to acknowledge that and other brutal facts of life has a way of resonating with those who are on the receiving end of the message.

I've already alluded to the power of humor and laughter in conveying a message. Laughter has a way of opening people up, tearing down walls, and enabling us to receive the truth of a message that's coming our way. It is good for the mind, body, and spirit to laugh. As Norman Cousins said many years ago, laughter is "inner jogging." It has a positive effect on our lives, and I think it belongs in worship because I'm convinced that God must have a sense of humor. After all, you and I are created in God's image, and we have been given the gift of laughter and humor by God. We need to use it.

That means that almost all of our services involve something that's lighthearted and humorous. It is not always in the spoken message, but it could be in a humorous video clip or in a fun song. Sometimes it is in the interplay between worship leaders and congregations. For instance, when we mess something up, we point it out and laugh about it. One Sunday, the lights went out in the middle of my message. All I could think to say was, "Hmm, I wonder what that means." The sound was fine, and the slides supporting my message were all in order, so I kept on. Everyone laughed at the comment and then refocused on what we were talking about. Within a matter of a minute, the lights came back on, and everyone cheered.

Likewise, on a Sunday when I was at our second site, our timing didn't coordinate very well, and our transmission to Beef and Boards was delayed. The meditation slides were running; the keyboard was "vamping" (underscoring the silence with musical chords), and I was waiting. One thing I've learned is that I am not to begin my message until the lights come up, and then I'm supposed to count, "one, two, three," before beginning my sermon just to make certain all systems are go.

On this particular Sunday, the delay was extensive, and I waited prayerfully in the dark for maybe twenty seconds. As the time dragged on, the congregation became a bit restless, and I glanced at them and then returned to watching the slides. More seconds passed, and I sort of smiled and shrugged at those gathered in the room. Eventually, I did a little "soft shoe," and then one of the other hosts at Oak Hill came up, and we did a dance. Everyone smiled and chuckled. After what seemed like an eternity, the lights came up, and the whole Oak Hill congregation cheered and applauded. All I could think to say to the Beef and Boards crowd that had just joined us was, "Where in the world have you been? What have you been doing over there?" We all laughed and then settled into the rest of the service. Laughter is a wonderful gift, and it lifts a worship experience to new heights.

I've already mentioned the importance we place on inclusiveness, and we attempt to model that in everything we say and do. I try to be conscious of including everyone in my message. For instance, on Mother's Day, we acknowledge that not everyone is a parent (and we tend to use the word *parent* rather than *father* or *mother*), but that all of us have had a mother in our lives. I am also certain to include the fact that not all parents have been good ones, and so our role models may not be stellar.

The same thing is true when we mention coupled relationships. I usually use the word *partner*, rather than *husband, wife,* or even *spouse.* That is primarily because we have a sizable number of gay and lesbian couples who feel very much that The Garden is their spiritual home, and we honor and recognize the commitment they have made to each other. We show that spirit in the language we use.

Likewise, we are careful about the images we use to identify God. You will not hear God addressed as *Father* by any speaker at The Garden, and we will change that wording in a song if the song is exactly right for a part of the service, but refers to God as male. We don't use male pronouns in reference to God, and we will rewrite the Bible passage to avoid such usage. Although some would probably consider that blasphemous, we really believe that's the way the Bible would have been written if it had been composed today. We believe that God's will for us is continually being revealed, and we believe greater inclusiveness is part of that continuing revelation.

Furthermore, as a female in the Church and in society, I have become aware of the violence noninclusive language can do in subtle ways. I am committed never to inflict that kind of violence on anyone else. Many make fun of being "politically correct," but I believe that in order to honor the dignity and worth of *every* human being, we must be inclusive in every possible way.

One of the ways we have attempted to break down the walls when it comes to church is to avoid the traditional trappings of the church. We do not use church hymns, nor do we include any litanies or liturgy in our services. We do include baptism and communion as part of what we do, but we make sure that we do it in "The Garden way." I'll discuss later how that looks.

Another way we eliminate some of the trappings is that, as I hope you would expect, we do not wear robes or use a pulpit. Attire is casual for everyone, and I typically wear slacks and a sweater. Part of the reason I wear a looser top is to conceal the wires and pack for the body microphone I use at both locations. To avoid using any kind of a stand for my Bible, which contains the sermon, I simply hold it in my hands. This serves to remove any barrier between me and the congregation, and I think it creates more openness.

I will talk in a few moments about the actual details in preparing and delivering a message, but I'll share just a few hints that have worked for me. First, I do my best to make sure the sermon is given in a conversational style. I try hard not to alter my voice inflections or fall into that sing-song preaching pattern that some pastors have. I always use *I* or *we* and seldom use *you*. *You* sounds "preachy," and first person is more typical of our normal conversations. I do prepare a written manuscript of the sermon, but I do not memorize it, nor do I read it. It is my desire to be familiar with it, so familiar that, if I need to read a quote, or if I lose my train of thought, I know exactly where to look on the page and find a prompt. I also try to be so accustomed to the message that I know when to turn the pages without having to look down. This allows me to maintain eye contact with the congregation and enhances the conversational mode of delivery.

I've also found it helpful to use all the visual reinforcement I can during my message. We sometimes divide a sermon into segments to increase its "listen-ability." We will use songs or video clips, even congregational activities, to split the message and increase its appeal. After all, people have to be drawn in to hear what is being shared. The speaker is shown on screen, and I believe that this allows the attendees to view the speaker much more clearly than would be possible otherwise. I do notice that many eyes are on the screen rather than directly on the person who is speaking. Any quotes or key words I use appear on screen as they are spoken, and a quotation sheet is available at the doors and at the information tables each week to reinforce the message that is delivered.

Coordinating the timing in order to reinforce the message visually takes time and effort, but I can assure you that it is well worth the effort.

One more thing that is different from the normal expectation for preachers is that the message is typically twelve minutes in length. This took some getting used to when we first began, but it was absolutely necessary because of the time restraints under which we operate in our borrowed facilities. As the years have passed, I have begun to realize that it probably takes more careful crafting to present a twelve-minute message than it does to present a thirty- or forty-five-minute diatribe. The story I just loved will have to go if it doesn't fit precisely into the direction we're going and the one point I'm trying to make in my message. This has required discipline, but I believe that most Gardeners would tell you that they appreciate the effort that's been made.

Now I'll offer some details about how I work as the primary preacher for The Garden. I believe that I must do my best to do my part as a team player and to allow the rest of the team members the time and resources they need to do their best. When it comes to preaching, I seek the input of the Worship Design Team before creating the message; and as soon as the first draft is completed, it is in the hands of those team members, as is the request for feedback and other ideas.

I try to allow ample time for sermon preparation, and my typical week (of which there are very few) sets aside Tuesday and Thursday for sermon work. As with most pastors, there are always interruptions to our schedules. Hospital calls, a crisis, or a funeral can make it necessary to alter my schedule. I also attend a St. Luke's meeting each Tuesday morning, and that sometimes delays my sermon preparation until later in the day.

On Tuesdays, I am usually studying and doing my research for the sermon that is three or four Sundays in the future. That is done in order to give plenty of preparation time for any creative ideas to germinate. If, for instance, today is Easter, my Easter message would have been completed and e-mailed to the Worship Design Team at least three weeks prior to today. The sermon I'm working on during Easter week is the sermon that will be delivered at least three weeks into the future.

I have heard many a preacher say, "Oh, I couldn't ever do that! I have to wait until the Spirit moves me!" I understand that sentiment, but I would argue that what typically turns out to be last-minute preparation leaves our paid and unpaid staff holding the short end of the stick. That's because they are asked to perform on short notice without adequate time to prepare well or to be creative. It simply is unfair, and I would go so far as to say unfaithful, for us to put those who work with us in that kind of situation. We must honor their private lives and the time of both our paid and unpaid staff and value the role they play in making each day meaningful.

On Tuesdays, I begin with prayer about the upcoming topic and then try to get out of the way to see where God leads. More often than not, the Holy Spirit is active, and the message takes on a life of its own. That means a very different direction from the outline I had created prior to putting the first word on paper. I've learned that the sermon will unfold if we truly trust God and do our part in the cocreation process.

A large part of my work is searching through files, looking for materials I've gathered that relate to the upcoming topic. Currently, I have six three-inch binders that I refer to as my "clip books." In them, I have articles from magazines or newspapers that I have "clipped" out and saved. I've also created an index, numbering each article, and giving it a brief description with one or two key words. All of the information from these books is updated frequently and is in a Word document so I can use the edit/find function to retrieve the materials that are relevant to my topic.

The same thing applies to the books that I read, and I read a lot! I've gotten in the habit of noting page numbers and jotting a description of what I've read inside the back of each book. That, too, is now in a Word document, and once again, I can search and find references to any number of other possible sources for material. In addition, members of the Worship Design Team are generous about sharing articles they cut out or read, and they're also good about sending me useful stories by e-mail.

My preparation process begins with prayer and asking God to direct me in the way I should go with this particular subject matter. Then I begin to read and study the Bible to find references to the topic. Following that, a search is conducted through my clip books and other books, and I note everything I find on notebook pages that are in another three-inch binder and dated by Sunday. Often in the process of researching one topic, I will happen upon something that fits an upcoming theme and can switch quickly and jot it down in that date's section of my notebook. It is my goal to complete this work and to have an outline of the message ready by the time I go to Worship Design Team on Tuesday evenings.

My Thursday work consists of actually putting the sermon together. As I mentioned earlier, I have gotten in the habit of writing a manuscript, primarily because that helps the other team members see the possibilities of dividing a message, or of how a song or movie clip might illustrate and fit within the sermon itself. Sermon writing usually takes me three or four hours, and once the first draft is completed, I e-mail it to everyone on the Worship Design Team and solicit their feedback.

Sermon work for the week isn't done with that e-mail. It then becomes time to proof and make any suggested changes to the message for the Sunday directly ahead. Once that is done, I mark all the quotes in red and e-mail that message to the Tech Team and to the person who is preparing the slides for the service. (The slide presentation, incidentally, is e-mailed to the tech team members by 5 P.M. on Saturday evening and is loaded either onto a CD by the team member, or directly onto The Garden's laptop computer for transport to The Garden the next day.) My administrative assistant also receives a finalized copy, which she proofs and formats to fit in the Bible I hold each Sunday. She gives that to me on Fridays.

Saturday morning is the beginning of the intensive work on the next day's message. I begin the day by recording the sermon onto a tape and listen to it much of the day, when I'm driving to and from church, walking, doing laundry, or pulling weeds. We try to keep Saturday evenings fairly quiet in our household, since Sunday is such an early morning. I spend at least an hour practicing my sermon aloud, trying to become familiar with where things are on the page, if I need a prompt. I do not memorize the sermon, nor do I read it. My goal is to make it a part of me and to be able to share it in a conversational way with Gardeners. It often changes in the course of my practicing it, and the transitions are usually much better and clearer because of the time spent in practice. The last thing I do on

Saturday nights before going to sleep is to listen to the tape of the sermon with the text of the message open in front of me.

Sunday begins at 5:00 A.M. for me. I shower and go into another area of the house to spend at least another hour in prayer and in practicing the message. Once again, this helps me be familiar with the message I'm going to share and builds my confidence level that it is well in mind. Once I am dressed, I leave the house by 7:00 A.M., and listen once more to the message on my way to the theater. On the Sundays that I travel to the 10:15 service at our second site, I listen to the sermon again in transit.

We have to be at the theater and with our microphones on by 7:30, because that's when we're all there to begin what we call our "cue to cue" rehearsal. It is a technical rehearsal that includes sound checks, running through the music and the slides, checking the video segments, and setting the camera for the transmission. At 7:55, we form a prayer circle with everyone who has been helping, and we open the doors at 8:00. Then we're on a roll, as we repeat our service three times each Sunday. Afterward, we assist the wait staff as needed, load everything back into the loading van, and transport it to our storage areas. After filing all the materials we used that day and noting their use on that Sunday, we're ready to start pushing the ball uphill again.

The message portion of our Sunday service can take several different forms. On most Sundays, it is delivered in one twelve-minute spoken segment, supplemented by visual reinforcement (quotes, pictures, and so on). On other Sundays, we may decide to divide the message into several parts and intersperse the segmented message with music or video clips. At times we have used other media—such as video specials or musical selections—as the heart of the message and threaded it together with the Bible passage or some other type of commentary. We are not wed to the spoken word as the only format for the sermon itself, although that is what we use most often.

In musical terms, each Sunday ends with a "reprise." That is, my closing, or what many churches refer to as the "benediction." It comes at the end of the service and is a short story, a quote, or perhaps a movie clip that summarizes our topic for the day. Its intent is to inspire Gardeners to go out into the world and live out their faith. The final words are almost always, "Have a great Sunday, and go in peace. Amen." When I am not physically present at one site or the other, one of the other team members usually delivers the closing segment, since we usually transmit only the body of the sermon to our sister site.

If you are interested in more details about the types of messages we use each week, or would like to read some of those sermons, you will find them on our Web site. The address is www.the-garden.org.

Questions for Consideration

1. What might help your preaching be more relevant to today's attendees?
2. What process do you use for sermon preparation? How might that be improved?
3. What steps are you taking to make your sermons better?
4. What are your primary functions as the preaching pastor?

CHAPTER 13

PRODUCE FROM
THE GARDEN

Every good garden produces something, and our Garden is no
different. What are the fruits of our labor? What has been produced that plants seeds of God's love and goes far beyond the
confines of our Garden?

Obviously, one thing we have been able to produce is a quality
worship service that works for us. Perhaps it would be helpful to
share with you a more definitive understanding of what a Sunday
service might actually look like. For an even better understanding, I
would suggest that you look at volume two of the Igniting Worship
Series *Helping and Serving*, which The Garden produced with Spirit
Films for Abingdon Press, published in 2003. This little book contains ten services that we have used at The Garden to encourage
Gardeners to help others.

In general, a typical service (although there isn't really a "typical"
service, since it changes every week) includes several basic elements,
and each element has its own unique function: to open the mind, to
touch the heart, to nourish the soul. We have discovered that using
more elements that are shorter is more effective than fewer long segments. What we would term our most successful services are likely
to contain fifteen or sixteen different parts that are put together into
a cohesive whole. Each Sunday's "flow" (written document detailing
the order of the elements in the service, the timing, and the responsible participants) is unique, depending on the elements we use. Our

creative director has a gifted eye and a wonderful sense of what flow creates the very best service, and we rely on her to put the finishing touches on the flow that is hammered out in our Worship Design Team meetings.

Each service focuses on a single theme, and every element of the service is connected to that theme, either in setting up the theme, or in transitioning or resolving it. It is our desire to create a well-integrated service during which everything fits together. We try to eliminate anything that fails to move us forward in the course of the service. Although sometimes that means losing the song we really wanted to sing or the story we wanted to tell, it does keep us focused on that particular morning's theme.

Sometimes, although not always, our theme lends itself to a clear visual image. For example, if we happen to be talking about planting seeds of God's love, seeds become our image. That image is reinforced as background for our slides; the band would sing songs with the word "seed" in them; we are likely to hand out packets of seeds as attendees leave the service. Seeds become the metaphor that shapes our service.

The flow of the service might look something like the following:

:30   Garden open/jingle/"Good morning, and welcome to The Garden"

1:00   Opening video clip to introduce the morning's topic

2:00   Intro/welcome (This sets the stage for the morning and helps people settle in. It is also used to invite Garden attendees to explore the ensuing theme with us. Brief announcements are also included here.)

4:00   Song 1, which introduces the topic again and moves us forward

2:00   Video clip that illustrates the theme

2:00   Prayer

3:30   Song 2, which moves the service along

2:00   Video clip that serves as transitional element

4:00   Song 3, which carries the theme forward

12:00   Message

2:00   Closing video clip that resolves the subject

4:30   Closing song that "nails" the topic

1:30   Closing/parting

You'll note that we schedule approximately thirty-six to thirty-eight minutes for the service, knowing full well that movement and transitions take up the additional two or three minutes we have to spare. Also, in the 10:15 service, a minute or two is allotted for "meditation slides" allowing the sites to get in synch for the live transmission of the message.

Special Services

There are three services each year that have presented the greatest challenge to us to do in "The Garden way." Those three are our Good Friday service, our newly created Easter sunrise service, and our Christmas Eve service. In fact, Christmas 2003 was probably the first time we came close to creating a service that was the kind of Christmas Eve experience a Gardener would have come expecting. I'll outline those services briefly.

Our Christmas Eve service has changed each year, but we think perhaps we have found a way to be "Garden-esque," yet embrace some of the traditions that people seem to find meaningful, even if they have no prior experience with a church. The key for us in 2003 was that we created a contemporary version of the Christmas story and used a reader's theater format for sharing the story. It was done in segments, the Luke version of the Christmas story interspersed with the scripture reading, as were numerous popular Christmas songs (not carols) that helped carry the story line.

My message on Christmas Eve was divided into three parts, with each part strategically placed to enhance the meaning of this special service. We have had a candle lighting experience since the first Christmas Eve service we ever offered, but again, we have to do it a bit differently at The Garden. Our tables are covered with green and red plastic cloths, and candles in plastic wine goblets are already on the tables when people arrive.

The lighting takes place after a special video, created new each year, using the Mannheim Steamroller version of "Silent Night."

During 2003, we began our service with a contemporary version of that familiar carol, and we also had a part of the service during which our children used sign language to accompany a recorded version of "Silent Night." Thus, that carol, familiar to most, was the thread that shaped our service, and it proved to be an effective way to form that particular experience.

Our Good Friday service is similar each year, and it is held at Beef and Boards at noon on Good Friday. The service tries to blend traditional images with popular music that gives a very different "feel" to the service. We begin with a short clip from the movie *Amistad*, and that is followed by prayer. Following that, the song "The Prayer" is sung; and then the story of the crucifixion, rewritten in narrative form, is read, interspersed with popular music such as "Tears in Heaven," "My One True Friend," "I Get Lost," "How Do I Live," "Streets of Philadelphia," "Higher," and "Fly." Attendees are handed a spike-like nail as they enter, and the service has become a very powerful setup to our Easter services.

Easter sunrise was a new service for us in 2004, and it is becoming a "signature service" for our Oak Hill family to host. The setting there is conducive to a sunrise service in the same way that the theater is an ideal setting for a Good Friday service. This was a very different service from that day's other four services and began in darkness, and included removing the black draperies from the windows with a young ballerina leading the procession in a ceremonious fashion. The music became bold and celebrative, and the service was uplifting and hope-filled. Dancers concluded the service in an upbeat way, and attendees took with them prisms to allow folks to see the light of day shining through what had been the darkness of night. It, too, proved to be quite effective.

I'll offer just a word about the times we offer communion and perform baptisms. Although many churches do it much more frequently, the United Methodist tradition calls for communion four times a year. We don't usually serve communion that often, but we always serve it during Lent and in early October. Both of those times, we create a theme that incorporates the communion service, that ensures that communion will be integrated into what we're talking about, and not be a disjointed part of the service unrelated to anything that has come before or that will follow. We vary the elements we use in communion, sometimes resorting to bread and juice, but more often trying to choose foods that help everyone become aware that Christ's presence is with us always, and not just with bread and juice or wine. We have used cookies and milk, doughnuts and apple juice, goldfish crackers and soft drinks, and a variety of other common foods to point out that the sacred is contained within the ordinary.

Again, baptism is done "our way." Typically, in our tradition, we are talking about infant baptism, although we also perform adult baptisms upon request. When we baptize a child, we make sure to choose a time when the theme supports the addition of baptism; that's done to make our service an integrated whole. That baptism occurs whenever it fits best with the flow of the service and the message—sometimes at the beginning, perhaps in the middle, and often toward the end.

The traditional words of baptism have been rewritten to fit our setting and belief system; and after the service of baptism, if the parents so choose, those in the congregation get the opportunity to offer their support and blessing. This is usually done while the band sings a song that fits the occasion, and we show pictures of the child with siblings and family on screen during the song while they are greeted by Gardeners. Again, the focus is on making the entire service a meaningful experience for everyone concerned.

Produce That Has Spread Beyond Our Garden

There are three outreach endeavors that have spread beyond The Garden into our community, across our country, and around the globe. In the next paragraphs, I will describe our 10% Charitable Contributions program, the project we refer to as "50/50," and our "1+1=1, The Power of One" undertaking.

The Garden sees itself as an outreach ministry, and we attempt to keep outwardly focused. That does not mean that we ignore the needs of our congregation, but it is not an either-or situation in our minds, but rather a both-and. We care for our own and constantly reach out to others, always in love.

I've given a little bit of information about our 10% Charitable Contributions program when I discussed our Charitable Contributions

Team. Several years ago, because of our belief in abundance, our Leadership Team elected to begin giving 10 percent of the money that comes to us in our watering cans each Sunday to a different grassroots charitable organization each month. For example, our recipient for April 2004 was an organization called Teachers' Treasures. This group receives school supplies from business organizations and then allows teachers from area schools to go on a shopping spree to purchase (at no cost) pencils, paper, art materials, and so on that the schools, teachers, or students cannot afford to purchase on their own. Our video team met with the leaders of the group, visited the facility on a shopping day, and interviewed teachers who, shopping carts in hand, were gathering some of their much-needed supplies. On a Sunday in May, a representative from the group came to The Garden to receive their check and a copy of the video that was created to help them spread the word and advance their fund-raising efforts with other funding bodies.

That's the scenario that unfolds each month. The Charitable Contributions Team collects suggestions from Gardeners and then conducts research on each group, selecting the twelve who will be our recipients during any given year. The team has set up some parameters for evaluating the group and their need for our financial gifts and has usually limited the geographic area from which the recipients come to the seven-county Indianapolis metropolitan area. Recently, an exception to that geographic limitation was made, and the recipient for May 2004 was an organization called Candles. This is a private Holocaust museum in Terre Haute, Indiana, that was created by a survivor of the Holocaust who, along with her sister, was a victim of the twins' experiments conducted in the Nazi concentration camps. Several months ago, that museum was destroyed by a fire that was set by an arsonist, and we are hopeful that our funds will assist in the attempt to rebuild and reopen the museum. Furthermore, our Garden Youth Group will make a trip to Terre Haute in the fall to be part of a work project in the rebuilding efforts. This is a good example of how we can help worthwhile area organizations help others, assist them in their fund-raising efforts, and provide hands-on opportunities for our Gardeners to be involved.

A second project that spread throughout our country and beyond is one we called our "50/50" project. This project is described more thoroughly in volume two of the Igniting Worship Series (*Helping and Serving)*, which The Garden prepared for Abingdon Press. A Gardener came to me with an idea. She wanted to give me $2500 and wanted me to give fifty Gardeners $50 each to go out and plant seeds of God's love in our world. How could they multiply their $50 and do good in this world? How could they make a difference in someone else's life?

The stories that came back were fascinating, as Gardeners enlisted friends and family to double, triple, or quadruple their funds; and we've captured those stories in a booklet entitled "Planting Seeds of Hope and Love." (If you are interested in reading some of those stories, please contact The Garden office at 100 W. 86th Street, Indianapolis, Indiana 46260, or phone 317-846-3404.)

Gardeners were quite imaginative in coming up with ways to make an important difference in the lives of others. One group of Gardeners created a petting zoo on their farm and invited inner-city preschoolers to come visit for a day. Another Gardener organized a golf outing for Special Olympic students, with each student paired with a Gardener. Everyone enjoyed a pizza party after their round of golf. Still another person from The Garden used the seed money to buy seeds and bulbs to help children at the school for the blind know the thrill of planting a flower garden. One couple turned her ailing father's farm into a production center for fresh produce for food pantries in Indianapolis.

I could go on and on telling the stories that came out of this experience, but even more important is that this idea didn't stop with The Garden. A feature writer for our Indianapolis newspaper wrote an article, and a writer for the Los Angeles *Times* picked it up. Before we knew it, it was a front-page story in many newspapers across the country, and the idea caught on. Other churches, businesses, and civic organizations began to realize how the pebble thrown in the pond has a ripple effect that touches countless numbers of people. The good that began with our "50/50" project continues to multiply today.

The last of the special projects I will discuss is one we're referring to as "The Power of One." It is based on our conviction that one person has the power to make a positive difference in our world. More specifically, we are committed to helping to eradicate HIV/AIDS in Africa. Our formula for the "Power of One" is this: $1+1=1$. I know that sounds like poor math, but we want everyone to know that *one* person can provide the means for *one* person with AIDS to live for *one* year. Basically, one dollar a day can provide the medication to save the life of someone suffering from AIDS in Africa. We are hopeful that this undertaking will spread to others, and one church can provide the means for the members of one church to live for one year; one community can provide the means for residents of one community to live for one year. And so it goes.

Furthermore, leaders of this endeavor have been able to make some important connections in our community to bring an additional dimension of the project into being. Indiana University School of Medicine has long had an exchange program with a university in Eldoret, Kenya, whereby students from Kenya can come to the medical school for training, and some of our trained physicians spend time helping in Eldoret. In the last few years, the focus of their work has been in effective treatment and in providing the educational and nutritional needs to end the blight of AIDS in that country.

We created a worship service in the fall of 2003 to raise the awareness of our Gardeners, and we were able to raise funds to donate to the IU/Kenya program for medication. Along with St. Luke's, the total contribution amounted to $50,000, but that wasn't the end. Someone who had become inspired by the possibility of making a significant impact offered a grant, making it possible to match the original $50,000, and giving the IU/Kenya project a donation of $100,000.

There were still funds left over to enable us to pursue a project we had dreamed about. Because of our talented video "gurus," we wanted to take the fall 2003 service mentioned above, shoot original footage, and create a documentary that could be used in churches and could be modified for schools and other organizations. That dream is becoming a reality. During the summer of 2004, we sent a crew from The Garden and St. Luke's to Eldoret, Kenya, to conduct interviews, shoot footage, and offer firsthand witness to the "Power of One." The team went to prepare a documentary that will be available during early 2005 for use in churches across this country. Together we hope to inspire others so that we can save thousands of lives.

As any good gardener knows, the harvest tells the worth of the gardening efforts, and we believe the same thing should hold true for our Garden. We are intent on being outwardly oriented, and we will extend ourselves so that we can "engage all in the quest to know and share" God's love. We can make a difference in this world by planting seeds of hope and love. Each one of us has the power to make this world a better place—10%, 50/50, the Power of One.

Questions for Consideration

1. If you were starting from scratch to create a worship experience, where would you begin? What would be essential ingredients in your service? What usual elements might you eliminate? What new parts would you add?
2. Design a service flow. What would begin the service? How do you want it to end? What would the central theme be?
3. What are new ways to spread God's love beyond the walls of your church? Where do the congregation's passions lie? How can we help our congregations live out their passions?

CHAPTER 14

WE WON'T PLANT THAT AGAIN!

When I chatted with our Lead Team (composed of six key staff members) about things that we would never do again, Suzanne Stark, our Creative Director and director of the Good Earth Band, quickly replied, "Sing 'Before the Parade Passes By!'" Her response reflected the kind of music we relied on in the very early days. Since her training is in music and theater, and since she and her husband own Beef and Boards Theater, her focus was on Broadway musicals, or show tunes. The band used to tease her constantly about some of the music she chose in the first six months of our existence, and yet there is a very real sense in which that path was the one we had to walk before we could get to where we are now. Because of that early shaping experience, her range of musical interest broadened, and the type of service we currently offer was created.

That's one way of saying that we won't be afraid in the future to try new things, to branch out. Sometimes our tendency is to rely on what we already know and keep doing what we're doing. We know it "works," and success is an easy trap. We have made a commitment not to rest on our laurels and play it safe, but to keep "pushing the envelope." One of the things we want never to do again is to live in our comfort zone.

Be in Control

On a more basic level, what is it that we will never do again? What things will we not try to plant again? My first response is that we will not try to be in control of everything. In several of our efforts, we have tried to force things to happen, and it just didn't work. At one point in time, we thought that we needed to have a building of our own or, even more ambitious, that we needed to own a shopping center to provide income and a home for The Garden. We talked to developers, contractors, business leaders, and church leaders; and for probably a good year, we invested a great deal of time and energy trying to make some physical home of our own happen. Nothing worked right. We were stymied at every juncture and became disillusioned and frustrated.

Finally, we had a "come to Jesus" conversation and realized that we were trying too hard to *make* something happen. In other words, we had quit listening to God and were listening instead to our own voices. Certainly, I believe God works through each and every one of us, but in this instance, that was not the voice of God. Rather, it was our own egos and selfish desires.

Once we were able to let go of our need to control things and let God lead, some surprising things once again began to happen. It became clear that we weren't about owning things, but instead we were about using preexisting space during hours that the host enterprise wasn't using it. It was a much wiser use of our resources; and when we finally let go, additional space became available. We had been looking so hard in one direction and one direction only, that we simply couldn't see the other possibilities that were lying right before our eyes.

Trying to be in control has been an issue for us more than once. We have tried to force other things to happen—a children's program, for example, and it failed. Why? Because the timing wasn't right, and our thinking was not ready. We had fallen back into more traditional ways of thinking, and we weren't being creative. We tried to create something that nobody wanted or was ready for. Our Gardeners did not know that a children's program was a normal and expected part of church. Only recently has a team of those passionate about kids and about their getting the message in "The Garden way" stepped forth.

On Easter 2004 The Garden Kids programming was launched. It's going like gangbusters! That's because the leaders are creating materials that coordinate with the theme each week and are preparing a "Garden-to-Go" menu for families to take with them to reinforce the message everyone has received and absorbed during the morning.

In essence, what I'm saying is that it is important that we not try to control everything about the ministry we want to create. Most of the time, it is essential that we step aside and "let go and let God." If we trust that God will not lead us astray, and if we sincerely try to listen to God's voice and follow, we cannot fail. That's been one of the greatest lessons I've learned over the past nearly ten years. When we trust God and God's timing, the right things will emerge, converge, evolve, and unfold. I suppose that's what I mean when I refer to The Garden as being organic. Things have happened in God's timing and, I pray, in God's way. We promise to be good team players on God's team, but we will not "hog the ball."

That's not to say that we don't plan and do our best to live out our plans. It is to say that we prayerfully consider what God has in mind and then attempt to work in accord with God's direction. Do we have a strategy plan? Yes, we do, and that plan was carefully put together by faithful Gardeners four or five years ago. It contains eight basic emphases for The Garden; and with the exception of the space portion, we keep moving positively in the direction of living out that plan. However, we have not met the date criteria we set when the plan was developed. That has been where God's timing has entered in. It seems that our plan is on target, but our time factor for bringing the plan to fruition has not been.

Small Groups

There's another thing we won't try again: we will never again try to plant small groups the way we did at the very beginning. Even though that kind of thing works well in many, many churches, it was not effective for us. We were trying to follow the typical model of creating small groups—the kind of groups I watched in action when I traveled to Korea. However, that simply did not work for us. We neglected to notice that groups form best around affinity, and we were attempting to design every element of the group. It was just too artificial for us. It also wasn't true to who we are as a congregation; the groups we tried to start weren't really reflecting the DNA of The Garden.

Again, we have tried to encourage relationship building in a number of ways, and we have waited patiently to see what would happen. It has been slow in developing, due to the Disney-like environment we have at the theater (in the front door and out the sides with fifteen minutes between services). However, as teams have grown, connections between Gardeners have been made and friendships have been created. Our bands would be one example of the kind of relationships that are formed when people work together to achieve a common goal. Other groups are springing up out of Gardeners' desires and needs, not because we think they ought to be in small groups. Again, by nurturing the seedlings, we are seeing the kind of things happen that we hoped for but were unable to orchestrate and choreograph into being.

Drama

Another item that we have had to drop except on occasion is drama. It probably sounds surprising that a church that meets in a working theater doesn't have a drama team. We have been surprised by that, too. We never dreamed that our video would be such a strength, and live drama such a growing edge for us, and yet it is. Again, at the beginning, we used several of the drama sketches that we purchased from Willow Creek Church in Chicago, but they met with varying amounts of success. Often, we had to rewrite because we found them too conservative theologically for us. Obviously, many others use them much more successfully than we were able to. Unfortunately, our talent pool hasn't yet produced someone who has the passion and desire to write the kind of things we would find most useful.

I'm not saying that we don't use drama at all because that simply is not true. Let's just say that we're selective about what we use and who participates. We have a Gardener who, when he is available, makes a wonderful "Church Lady" and who is very good at interacting with the congregation and getting us all laughing at ourselves and at him. We have some other characters who present themselves from time to time; and when appropriate, we try to use them. We have used cast members from Beef and Boards productions to reproduce a scene for us, and we use some of our talent resources in making our original videos. To say that we don't use drama is really not accurate. More accurate is to say that we do not use drama in a traditional way. We use drama if we think it will fit, rather than trying to force the drama into the service. One more commitment we have made about drama and every other element of our service is this: if we can't do it well, and if it doesn't fit in what a particular Sunday theme is about, we won't do it.

Copying Other Churches

Another thing we tried early on, but quickly discarded, was trying to pattern ourselves after the way other churches were functioning. It would have been easy to do what everyone else was doing, and that was seriously contemplated. However, it became clear that we were violating our own integrity by trying to be someone else. Trying to copy exactly what someone else was doing was not being who we are. It was not being authentic; it was not being true to ourselves and to God, nor would it be using our best strengths and resources. The ways other churches use work for them because they reflect the character of that congregation and they use the gifts and strengths that are present in that context. It took some time to figure out what we were to be about, but once we cleared our vision of other churches' ways of being church, we had much greater success at seeing what God had in mind for us!

One of the first ways we were able to sort that out was by attending an evangelism conference at Community Church of Joy in Phoenix. This was in April before The Garden actually began the following September. At that time, the conference was called "Reaching the Unchurched," and because Joy is a mainline denomination church (ELCA), we felt their team might have more to say to us than, for instance, Willow Creek. That part was right.

Our music director and I attended the conference together, and it was excellent. It was not top-notch because they told us we needed to do exactly the same thing they were doing. Instead, it was superb because they presented issues that caused us to think for ourselves, and they asked all the right questions. As we experienced their worship, we were able to think, "We could do that.... However, we'd do it *this* way." We found ourselves saying, "We wouldn't feel comfortable doing that, but we could do this." Although I've never been one to "follow the book" on what to do and how to do it, this conference freed us to consider new things, discard some things—both new and old—brainstorm other ideas, and adapt or modify some things. It empowered us to create our own way of being Church, and I am extremely grateful to Joy and to their leaders for making themselves available and vulnerable so that others of us can grow and learn.

Band Formation

Our bands began and continue to be mostly volunteer, but there's something concerning our bands that we would do differently if we were starting over. At the beginning, no one really had to audition. We just needed people and really appreciate the willing spirits who helped us launch. What we didn't know at the beginning was the amount of time, effort, and growth it would take to keep up with the band as it steadily improved in quality and commitment.

We also were not aware of the potential issues that could arise because of voices that do not blend well, or of personalities that do not mix with other personalities. Certainly, auditions might not have prevented all of the complications that have arisen, but they might have prevented some of them.

Making some of the mistakes we made in the early days has taught us a lot. One thing is the value of failure. We learn from it and continue to grow. It's important that we not be so afraid of failure that we fail to try anything. We must step out in faith, get up when we fall, and try again. If we keep getting up each time we fall, we will eventually be able to stand tall, with God's help. I'm convinced of it.

Questions for Consideration

1. What are some things you would never do again? Why would you not do them again?
2. Think about the mistakes and failures of your congregation. What has happened as a result of the failures you've noted? How has everyone learned from the mistakes?
3. What would it mean for your congregation to get out of the way of God's leading? Where do you think you might go, and what do you think you might do? Why are you still sitting here?

CHAPTER 15

GARDENING TIPS

Many congregations that are considering a new way to be church have contacted us over the years for tips and ideas of what works and what doesn't. I always try to caution each person or group to whom I speak to take what we say and put it into their hopper of ideas and possibilities. We certainly don't have all the answers, and we've made our fair share of mistakes, some of them very painful mistakes.

However, there are some things we have been fortunate enough to learn that may be helpful to others who are starting out. My intention for this chapter is to share some of the questions we have been asked and to give a sampling of our thoughts.

What have been some surprises for The Garden?

I usually share three surprises that have had the greatest influence on me. First is the use of tables for those in attendance. In my teaching days, I didn't want anything between me and my students. My room was always arranged in a semicircle, and my desk was in the back of the room. I never wanted to stand behind a desk and teach, because I felt that the desk would be a barricade to making a connection with the class.

I have to admit that, when The Garden began at Beef and Boards Dinner Theater, I was apprehensive about everyone having to be seated around the tables, which are permanently installed in the theater. Even though the theater is tiered, I feared that the tables would somehow get between us, but I was wrong.

Instead, the tables offer a level of comfort and community that we couldn't have any other way. I would never "do church" without tables again! It is interesting to see the way people bring their food to the table, begin chatting with one another, and then hold one another's hands during the prayer time. People meet one another more easily, and yet they also have the option of sitting off by themselves. I think it's important that we not violate that privacy. People seem to gravitate toward one another, and it's been amazing to see how certain families or groups of friends always seem to sit in the same place each week. The tables that start out with one or two persons at them gradually get to the point where there are three or four or more. When that happens, community-building begins to happen.

Second, I had become accustomed to the tradition at St. Luke's, worship services running concurrently with church school for children. That means that children were seldom or never in the worship service. When we began The Garden, that's what we expected to happen, but that isn't the way it unfolded.

Shortly after we began, we noticed that more and more families were joining us and that their kids weren't going to child care or to the children's program we had so carefully designed. They were choosing to sit in the service with their parents. Then we started to hear comments such as, "Sunday at The Garden is the only time we sit down at a table together as family during the entire week." We heard: "The kids get it, too! We talk about the same thing in the car on the way home, and they even bring things up later in the week."

That was a new discovery for us. Probably because we were fast paced and casual, kids were happy being there. In fact, more and more we hear how it's the kids who decide that the family is going to church each week. We don't really direct the service to kids but try to make the point we want to make so clear that people can't miss it. Apparently, that's true for children, too.

Third, again, I made some assumptions about the persons who would make their home at The Garden, and I was surprised by those who have. In the early days, we didn't make any special effort to build diversity into the makeup of our congregations, but that has happened naturally. As stated earlier, we were intent on reaching "unchurched boomers," and they responded. However, they weren't the only ones who responded. We have all ages—from nine days to ninety years old! People of all colors and nationalities have made their home here. Those who have never been to church have become friends with those who have always been in the church.

You might be wondering why, and I wish I knew the answer to that question. One simple response might be that everyone is different, and "one size fits all" may not be the best approach. Another reply might be that some have always been uncomfortable in traditional church—for whatever reason—but this is the first time they've found an alternative way to be part of a church family. I suppose that others don't like to sing or participate in the typical church ways and are much more comfortable with a less participatory and more engaging style. Some who do not know church lingo respond to our "no prior experience required" threshold. Although the answer to this question remains a mystery, one thing is clear—a nontraditional ministry such as ours meets the needs of many in today's world.

What about membership?

For a variety of reasons, we do not offer the option of becoming members of The Garden. If anyone wants to "join" The Garden, he or she can do that by affiliating with St. Luke's United Methodist Church. So the option is available for those who choose it. However, we decided early on that we didn't want to create a "we-they" mind-set, and we tried to be very clear that we believed that every one of us is already part of the family of God. We're already "in," so to speak, and so there's no necessity to join. In addition, there seems to be a trend away from joining organizations these days, and some do not find reason to join. I have no data to back up this next hunch, but I suspect that some of the recent publicity around organized religion has served to taint its image, thus making "joining" less desirable.

Do we pay our musicians?

The short answer is no. A more accurate detailed response is that we have always paid the directors of our bands, and we have always paid our keyboardists. The new band at Oak Hill has used the money allotted for a second keyboardist to hire a couple of instrumentalists who play regularly, and that consists of a drummer and two guitarists. However, the rest of our band members are unpaid servants who are passionate about music and about sharing God's love in unconventional ways.

Why don't people participate more?

If one just attends a service at The Garden, I'm sure the difference between what happens there and what happens in a typical "contemporary" service would be noticeable. Most of the time, our attendees do not sing with the band, and we seldom say things together. What many traditional churchgoers think of as participation is typically standing up to sing a hymn or to repeat the words to a creed. Over the years, I have found traditional church rituals, whatever they may be, less and less personally meaningful.

Instead of "participation," we have elected to talk about "engagement." It is our goal to engage Gardeners at the core of their being— their hearts and minds and spirits. We want the worship experience to touch their souls and change their lives. That is not something that can be measured by "participation" in a service.

What are the most important things to consider in creating a worship experience to reach new people?

This would be my list of important ingredients:

- Hospitality that welcomes, but does not smother. I mean something that is warm and inviting, provides a sense of comfort that creates a pleasant environment, and respects the worth and dignity of each person.
- Music that "works" and connects with those who attend. It is extremely important that the music be top quality and communicate what we are trying to say.
- A message that's relevant. That means being in touch with what people are experiencing in life and reflecting that awareness in our preaching. It also means offering hope and possibility, and not "beating people up" for their faults.
- A site that's nonthreatening. A secular location is more welcoming to some than is a church building, but even a

church setting can be made pleasant with the appropriate décor—flowers, candles, and so on—the use of appealing music upon entering, and comfortable places to sit.

- Following God's lead, rather than doing it because everyone else is. We always say, "This must be a 'God-thing,' because we're too inept to be able to do this on our own." There's no way something like this works unless it is of God.
- Staying outwardly focused. It's important that we reach beyond our doors to share the most important message people will ever hear. We must concentrate on reaching out and engaging others in the Great Commission.
- Being open and inclusive and accepting and nonjudgmental. This means meeting people where they are, and not assuming where they must be or must go to "qualify" for church. It's important not to condemn, but to encourage and accept all people from every corner of the world.
- Focusing on empowering others. I'm talking about sharing ministry, and not seeking power or status or rank for ourselves. I have already discussed this in the chapter on teamwork, but let me repeat the essence of what I mean. We work together in an egalitarian way. We are without a hierarchy or "pecking order" of importance of the individual or contribution. Everyone is worthy and adds a great deal to The Garden.

What warnings or cautions do we have to offer?

I have several cautions to share with others who are considering such an undertaking. They are:

- This is labor-intensive. It takes hundreds of hours each week to make something like The Garden happen, and it doesn't cease. We haven't yet found a way to shortcut most of the work, and when we have tried, everything falls short.
- Be clear on priorities. We can't do it all, and we cannot be all things for all people. It's important to streamline and set our priorities and stick to them.

- Take time away. In order for any ministry to be effective and meaningful, we who are leaders must care for ourselves. We can't be good to others unless and until we are good to ourselves. That means being healthy and striving for wholeness. It means staying in touch with the Source, being spiritually centered, and living true to our own personal mission statement. We need to realize that our need for spiritual connection varies from time to time and varies by age and stage.
- Find support. Launching a creative enterprise can be a lonely place, and sometimes some hurtful criticisms can bring us down. That's why it's important to create a support system of those who are in tune with us and whom we can trust. Those are the ones we can turn to and can be open and honest with about our hopes and dreams and fears.
- Prepare for surprises. I've mentioned three of the surprises for us, but to reiterate, they're the use of tables, the children's ministry, and the diversity of those who responded to this type of ministry. It's been amazing to discover what can happen when God works in and through ordinary people like us. It's also amazing what can happen when we don't care who gets the credit.

What do we do about those who resist anything new like this?

Frankly, I don't know the answer, because we really didn't experience much of that resistance. I suspect that has to do with the fact that we didn't take anything away; we were adding to. That is very much part of who St. Luke's is because that congregation has always added new ministries at an exponential rate. Also, we were off-site, and sometimes it is "out of sight, out of mind." To some degree, we stayed under the radar and just did our own thing.

I realize that isn't always possible. Many times, church people are resistant to change, and I suspect that's mostly out of fear of loss. It may also happen when church members do not hold a clear vision for the purpose of the church. If we are living true to the Great Commission, it seems to me that our focus needs to be on reaching those who are outside the church, and we must find creative ways to do that.

Resistance seems to happen most often when we try to change existing services, or even just the time of a service. My guess is that the key is how the proposed changes are introduced, and how invested people feel in the decision-making process. Whatever you do, do not begin unless and until you have the support of the congregation. Many from St. Luke's UMC tell us, "This is not for me, but we support what you're doing 100 percent." That's the kind of support we need.

What about staffing?

We began The Garden with a music director, a keyboard player, and one part-time clergyperson—me. Everyone else was unpaid staff, or more affectionately known as volunteers. I've outlined how our staff has grown to what it is now, but we continue to rely heavily on our volunteers to carry the bulk of the ministry. During the first two years, I transitioned from part-time to full-time, and my time at St. Luke's was redirected to The Garden.

How do you keep the relationship with the mother church?

We work at it. It's essential to build a relationship of trust between the leadership of both entities, and there must be mutual respect. There have been some difficult moments, to be sure, but both the senior pastor at St. Luke's and I work hard to keep our communication going and information flowing. He and I meet monthly for lunch, and someone from our team regularly attends a weekly meeting at St. Luke's to share pertinent details.

How many of your Gardeners really commit to the church? How do you measure this?

I'm not sure what "really commit" means. Are we talking about attendance? Membership? Mission? I suspect that, for most traditional churches, commitment to their churches is represented by membership figures, although those figures tend to be inaccurate and misleading. Since The Garden doesn't do membership, that doesn't work for us.

At St. Luke's, we've always believed that attendance figures are more reliable in assessing the level of commitment to our congregation. If we use that measurement for The Garden, I would have to answer that approximately seven hundred or more persons are committed to The Garden, as indicated by weekly attendance.

If we want to talk about financial commitment, we don't really expect those who attend The Garden to provide our entire financial support. If we try to figure out the dollar-giving average per attendee each week at The Garden, our figures point to about a five-dollar average. I don't know how that compares to the traditional congregation, but I would assume that it is low.

If we want to talk about levels of involvement in The Garden, I would have to respond that our involvement is extremely high. A large portion of our congregation is involved on a weekly basis with the work of The Garden, and many are involved in their own ministries beyond The Garden. In the spring of 2004, we challenged Gardeners to "act now" and provided opportunities for them to go out and, in a few hours' time, gather tools for a regional work project ministry and shop for children's toys and craft supplies for the pediatric ward in Eldoret, Kenya. More than 130 people showed up at six o'clock that Sunday evening with their tools and toys to gather, to meet others, and to celebrate the afternoon of helping others. Many more got tools and toys and brought them during the following week because they weren't able to join us that evening. I'd say that measures up to commitment to The Garden.

The hundreds of stories we hear regularly tell us of the commitment of Gardeners to making the world a better place. They go out into their schools, workplaces, and homes and live out their faith. For me, that is the greatest evidence of commitment to God and commitment to their spiritual home.

How do you know people are actually growing in their faith?

My response to a question such as that one is that only God knows how someone, anyone, is growing in faith. That's not something for me to judge in someone else. We do not adhere to the traditional formulas that many maintain as qualifications to be a "real" Christian. Those are more typical of a different style of Christianity from the one we profess at The Garden. Hopefully, we are providing the seeds for spiritual growth, and those seeds are nurtured by many opportunities for learning and growth. St. Luke's is a full-service church, and we at The Garden do not feel it necessary to reproduce all the ministries and study opportunities that are open and available to anyone who wants to participate at St. Luke's. Some Gardeners choose to participate in the Bible studies or book studies there; some participate in the work projects that both St. Luke's and The Garden offer. Others get involved in hands-on ministry through some of our charitable contribution recipients; most, if not all, pray on a daily basis. It is my feeling that they are growing in their faith in a way that suits who they are and what their needs are. What is important is their need for spiritual growth, and not our judgment on how they should grow in their faith.

I'd like to know if you pay apportionments.

Technically, no. The Garden separately is not a recognized church in our annual conference. However, we are a satellite of St. Luke's United Methodist Church; I am a pastor appointed to St. Luke's, and our attendance counts as a part of St. Luke's attendance. Therefore, we pay apportionments because St. Luke's does. I've already talked about the sums that St. Luke's pays in support of our conference and denomination, and they are sizeable.

What technical equipment do we need to offer a service similar to yours?

The basic answer to that question is as much or as little as you can afford, and the cost can range from $5,000 to $1,000,000. There are some basics that must be in place. They include a computer with software that's capable of generating slides. It can be PowerPoint, but it doesn't have to be. Another basic ingredient is an LCD projector to project the images on a screen, which is also a necessary purchase. The projector needs to be powerful enough to be seen in spite of potential lighting issues in the venue.

It's possible to use several television sets to project images, or a congregation could use an overhead projector. I would not recommend either. People today are too used to seeing projection that's professionally done, and an overhead would be inadequate to the task. Television sets would also have limited application, and it would be necessary to purchase several to do the job.

Good sound equipment is also a must, and it's probably helpful to work with a professional to determine the exact needs for a particular setting. We find it helpful to use body microphones for speakers, and handheld microphones for our vocalists. I would go so far as to suggest that it's important to have a trained professional run the sound each week. If there is someone who happens to be an expert in the field and who wants to volunteer, that's great! Otherwise, plan on spending the money to get good sound. It's essential.

Depending on what is being planned, a congregation might also consider purchasing such things as a camera to show the participants on screen, lighting to create the environment, and video editing software or equipment. These are added extras, but each one will make a contribution toward enhancing the service you want to offer. These items are totally dependent on the desired end result.

Question for Consideration

1. What other questions would you like to have answered?

CHAPTER 16

COULD WE PLANT A GARDEN, TOO?

Let's suppose that you have read to this point in the book, and you keep thinking, "Yes! I like it. We could do that!" If you were to come to me and ask me, "How do we start a Garden?" I would probably respond, "You don't." The reason I would answer that way is that I do not feel that anyone should try to replicate exactly what we are doing. I just don't think that approach proves to be successful in the long run. Even though it might seem easier at the beginning, it begs wrestling with some of the essential questions such as the *why*'s and *how*'s of being church. I would much prefer that each congregation debate those questions, come to consensus as to how they're being led, and then determine what pieces they can pick and choose to incorporate into their being. In essence, I'm talking about knowing who we are and living true to that identity.

Each congregation is unique, and every context is different. Although there is a plethora of basic elements of The Garden that are transferrable, the context into which they are used has a way of influencing the ultimate outcome. A case in point is The Garden at Oak Hill, our sister site to The Garden at Beef and Boards.

When we began Oak Hill at the beginning of 2003, we were able to jumpstart the new satellite because of our previous experience with Beef and Boards. We were operating by trial and error at the start of Beef and Boards; but by late 2002, we were clear on the personnel and the type of equipment we needed to create what The Garden does on

Sundays. We already had teams in place to coordinate various aspects of the bigger ministry of The Garden, and we could add additional team members from the new site to help broaden the scope of our thinking. We were not starting from scratch. This prior experience certainly was an advantage when it came to launching the second site. Instead of nine intense months of planning, we spent three to four months working out the arrangements.

However, we have discovered since the launch of The Garden at Oak Hill that the two sites, although aligned in our mission and our core values, have taken on very different personalities. Our services are parallel because we transmit the spoken message each week by live transmission. We have a dedicated T-1 line in place, and we coordinate the services by being careful about our timing, by watching the service at the other site, and by cell phone communication.

Even though the services are almost always identical, each site is distinct. The setting at Oak Hill has an influence on the congregation, and on the "feel" of the service. For instance, at Oak Hill, the tables are all round and seat six to eight persons. Even with the blinds pulled for better screen viewing, it is much brighter in the banquet hall than it is at Beef and Boards with all the work lights on. That affects the climate that attendees experience as they worship. It seems that Gardeners have connected with one another more quickly at Oak Hill than at Beef and Boards, and I suspect it is primarily because of the larger tables and brighter room.

I use the example of starting our second site to illustrate how different the two can be, even when the intention is to have one be an exact copy of the other. My caution to you, the reader, is to avoid trying to copy what someone else is doing. I'm hopeful that you have found some good ideas and useful tools within the pages of this book—tools and ideas that you can modify and shape for your context and setting. I think that is essential—to take in as many ideas as possible, and then to begin the process of weeding out those that just don't seem to fit who you are and what you're about.

Having said all that, I do have some suggestions about proceeding if there is within you an urge to try something new and different in your congregation. The first suggestion is an obvious one, and it's this: surround the idea that's taking form with prayer. When the dream on the airplane got my attention, that's all I could do! It was important for me, and for all of us, to keep trying to discern what the urge or idea or dream is all about. How might it take shape? Is it just a passing notion? How convincing and compelling is the urge?

If, after much prayerful consideration, we are still convinced that this is the direction in which God is leading us, I would suggest sharing it with a few trusted friends and colleagues. Try out the idea, and test the responses. Are there valid objections that should be considered? Are the reasons for doing this sound? Are the resources available to launch a new venture?

One of the most common reasons I hear for congregations starting a new style of worship service is because the big church in their city or town does it that way, and look what's happening there! That must mean that we should do the same thing. I'd say to be very careful of this reason for starting a new service or a new ministry of any kind. Ministries that begin with this rationale seldom succeed, and that's primarily because the passion is missing. Just because someone else is doing it and drawing people to their cause is not sufficient reason to do the same thing. Only if a congregation is convinced that a new direction is where God is leading, only if there are passionate people committed to make it happen, only if the resources are available to provide a quality offering, should that congregation continue the process.

I'm suggesting that perhaps the question really isn't, "How can we start a Garden, too?" Instead, I wonder if the better question isn't, "What can I do in this setting to improve our ministry?" I've always liked the Japanese word *kaizen*. It's a word that we find in many business books and journals, and it means "continual improvement." I can't find the original source of my introduction to this word, but as I recall, it had to do with a company such as Sony and its production of the Walkman. In the course of that product's history, there have been countless models and versions of the Walkman, and that's because the company has been constantly improving and upgrading its product.

How I wish that were the case with the church! We seem to be content to keep doing what we've always done, and some of that isn't done very well. Improvement seems to be a lost cause in many of our congregations. I really believe that it isn't so much the style of worship that appeals to a worshiper, but rather the quality with which a service is done. All too often we are satisfied with mediocrity and sloppiness in our music and in the sermon.

It occurs to me that many of those who offer contemporary services seem to feel that contemporary means "unplanned and spontaneous." Although spontaneity is appealing to some and can be effective at times, I fear that it does not work well for a prolonged period of time. I would hope that every congregation always be in the process of evaluating its ministry and the effectiveness of that ministry and then be constantly striving to improve. If we are truly living out God's call on our lives, it seems to me that we can do no less than give our best.

After better preparation, we may find that adequate personnel and other resources are still not readily at hand. What then? Let's suppose that music is an issue for a congregation. In today's world, there are many musical resources available for sale, and at a very reasonable price. Music tracks are available from almost every music outlet; and with solid background music, one good soloist can make a huge difference in the musical offering of a congregation. If music is an issue in a congregation, there are many ways to improve that situation with minimal expense.

What do we do if preaching is the bigger void in our congregation? I fear this is more common than most of us preachers would like to admit. A lot of the preaching I hear is just simply not up to par. By that, I mean that all too often it is dull, boring, and irrelevant. We are wasting our members' valuable time if we fail to create a message that connects with the hearts, minds, and spirits of those in our congregation; and there are too many resources available on the Internet or through a variety of publications for us to have a failed effort.

In addition, some churches are exploring the possibility of purchasing—again at a minimal cost—a DVD or videotape of some of the excellent messages that are offered in a number of our churches across this country. With a worship host, one soloist, one person who can operate the equipment, and music tracks and a prerecorded message, any congregation can put together a quality worship experience.

Speaking of technical expertise, it would also take a lot to convince me that a congregation does not have someone who's interested in computers and technology. If invited and encouraged and empowered, both young and old might value adding a new dimension to worship through visual reinforcement. People receive a message in many different ways, and not just through the spoken word. If we can find ways to share the message in visual ways, I suspect more and more people will be reached with God's love.

In that regard, it's been interesting to watch what has happened at St. Luke's. As The Garden was beginning, so was a multimillion-dollar building project on the campus of the "big church." A new sanctuary was essential to the plan, and it included a magnificent $700,000 pipe organ. However, in the early planning, there was no consideration of a screen and projection equipment. By the time plans moved along, that changed, and a big screen was installed in the new sanctuary.

Today, if you visit a worship service at St. Luke's, you will find the words to the hymns and creed projected on screen, and heads no longer are facing downward toward the hymnal or bulletin, but upward toward the screen. In addition, the preacher is also projected on screen during the sermon. If we watch closely, most of the congregation is watching the screen because the image is bigger than life and much easier to see for those further back in the sanctuary.

Although there was some grumbling early on about the use of the screens in worship, most of that has subsided. Many appreciate the additional service that's being provided, and even those who object the most grudgingly admit that they catch themselves watching the screen more than they thought they would. The voices of those who are visual rather than auditory learners are being heard, and the emphasis continues to be on how to share the message of God's love in a way that reaches more and more people.

Those are a few of the ideas I typically offer to anyone who seeks my counsel on starting a Garden. Whatever we do, and wherever we do it, it must be uniquely ours. Certainly, it contains the basic elements of good music and good preaching; but how those elements are shaped by our context and blended together is our challenge. The joy is in figuring that out and making it happen!

Questions for Consideration

1. How would an idea for something new be processed in your faith community? How would the leadership enlist support and "buy-in" by individuals and the larger faith community?
2. What resources are found in your congregation that could help create something different for your church? What variety of gifts is in your congregation?
3. What resources are you lacking? Where might you find those resources outside of your congregation?
4. What steps will you take to improve the ministry your church is currently offering?

CHAPTER 17

THE GARDEN TOMORROW

Wto be faithful to God's call on our lives. At this point, we believe it has
to do with living out our vision, our mission, and our core values;
and we believe that means using unconventional ways and always
trying to explore and create new ways of being "church."

I mentioned earlier that we have a strategy plan, and it still guides
the general direction in which we go. We are convinced it was put
together by a core of Gardeners who were trying to be faithful in
reflecting where God seems to be leading The Garden in the future.
Although we have missed most of the deadlines we had originally
set, the main sections of this plan continue to guide our actions.

I'll spend a few moments describing the contents of our strategy plan.

There are eight different categories represented in the nine-page
outline of the plan. They are as follows: Fellowship and Education,
Community Outreach, Virtual Church, Space, Exportable/
Transportable Products, Income Stream, Creative Partnerships, and
Three- to Five-Year Staffing Plan. Allow me to focus on each seg-
ment in more detail.

Fellowship and Education

When we modify and update our plan, I think we will suggest
another name for this section. It is really about how we help

Gardeners build quality relationships with one another and with God. Our goal is to create opportunities for spiritual, educational, and social connections among Garden children, youth, and adults. The reason this is a segment of our strategy plan is that it benefits the well-being of Gardeners by providing a greater feeling of connectedness, by building a knowledge base, by offering support, by creating a sense of belonging, by providing fun opportunities to gather together, and by offering avenues to grow in our faith.

Many features of this strategic element have happened, but they have happened because they have arisen from the needs expressed by Gardeners. Although our plan encompassed what has occurred, GYG (Garden Youth Group) came into being not because we said it had to happen. Rather, it began to take shape because a parent took the lead and created an offering for younger youth that was very much in the spirit of what The Garden believes and how it operates. It is not a traditional youth group in much of what it does, but is a way of further conveying the values we share.

The same thing is true of the recently formed Garden Kids—programming on Sunday morning for one- to twelve-year-olds. It came out of a need and developed after the leadership emerged, and it is Garden-like in its philosophy and theology. In the same way, an annual women's retreat came into being a couple of years ago. It, too, provides a means for getting away, growing spiritually, and meeting new friends, and that is especially important with having two sites and four different congregations.

At the Beef and Boards location, we were able to work out an arrangement with the building next door for renting space on Sunday mornings to facilitate our gathering together. Time to connect is minimal at Beef and Boards because of the schedule on which we must function with three services in a working theater. Therefore, we have space available next door that Gardeners reach by walking across a small bridge and following the path to the building. We call it "The Bridge." Our childcare is always there, and The Garden Kids meet there; but there are special offerings that draw more Gardeners and that create the potential for connections being formed. For example, this past Sunday, with the onset of summer in Indianapolis, we offered a farmer's market. Three or four vendors came, offering their produce for sale. In addition, a Sheltie rescue table was set up, and interested Gardeners could pursue securing a new pet through this rescue mission. Popcorn was available for everyone, and our Garden Market—selling shirts, visors, books, cards, and other Garden products—was also open.

Creating opportunities for relationship-building continues to be a challenge for us, and we continue to try to develop new ways that are more Garden-like to make that happen. Many parts of our strategic plan that pertain to this matter have come into being, but other ideas still need to be developed and more connections made.

Community Outreach

Another part of our strategy plan is community outreach. Expanded work in the community helps fulfill our mission. It reaches more people and increases the community's awareness of The Garden and its positive impact in our city. Our goal says that we want to promote the spiritual and social health of the community, and by that we mean both our own faith community and that of the greater Indianapolis community.

This has included expansion of our 10% Charitable Contributions program. At the outset, we were not able to provide a video to each organization, but we now make that a regular part of the gift each local group receives from The Garden. We are still aiming toward creating links from our Web site to theirs and enlisting more volunteers to help each organization in its effort to alleviate suffering and heartache in our world.

Another part of this plan has resulted in a form of partnership with various parts of the medical community in Indianapolis. Because we believe in a holistic approach to ministry, and because we believe that mind, body, and spirit are connected, we have offered numerous opportunities for Gardeners to check on the status of their physical well-being. Trying to promote good physical health has included offering flu shots on a yearly basis, as well as providing the opportunity for bone density testing. We still hope to make pedometers available and encourage Gardeners to walk at least ten thousand steps a day. With that promotion, we will also offer weekly weight and blood pressure monitoring.

One essential part of our outreach plan that hasn't been fully realized is the attempt to establish relationships with other faith paths and denominations. We explored this a bit during the summer of 2003 when I was away for a three-month clergy renewal leave. We had guest speakers from a variety of different faith persuasions, including a female Jewish rabbi. Our congregation responded in a positive way to this opportunity to expand our thinking and enhance our spiritual growth. We intend to pursue this approach to a greater degree in the future.

Virtual Church

A third portion of our strategy plan is called "virtual church." It is our goal to create a "Virtual Garden," although we are still not entirely certain what that looks like. It seems that the Internet offers tremendous possibilities for reaching a population that we would otherwise be unable to reach and furthers movement toward our mission and vision. Use of the Internet also makes it possible to improve our internal communication and allows us to share some of our resources with others.

We have made some progress toward our goal of creating the capacity to develop and enhance our Web site. Early in 2004, we hired a part-time person to improve our Web site and to keep it updated. We are still not interactive in video streaming our service, but we are now equipped for that to begin in the near future. All sermons are posted on the Web, and all of our communication publications are also available on the Web site. We hope to include discussion groups and online study opportunities in the future. Areas that we have not developed yet include a reference library of the resources we use, as well as databases of our music or of the basic content of the worship services we have already created. It seems to me that this is the new frontier for churches, and use of the Internet will be essential for all of us in the future.

Space

Our strategy plan originally called for buying or building a permanent facility, but our focus has changed since that plan was developed. We stated that our goal was to create a multi-use facility that would contribute to the long-term operation and ministry of The Garden. By that, we meant purchasing or building a structure that could be used during off times by other business or community entities. We discussed a conference center, a strip mall, a retreat center, a fitness center, and other such options. The intent was always not to look like a traditional church, either inside or out, and the hope was to cultivate secular partners who would rent the facility for their business needs and pay us for their use.

Since the plan was originally designed, this was the part that created the most conversation. Was it really being true to who we are to build even a nonconventional church building? Did it make sense to invest our financial resources in a business undertaking? How realistic was it to establish the partnerships that would make this possible? Although we developed a plan outlining our space needs, nothing else seemed to be unveiled that would make this possible. With the opportunity to go into a second site, our need for additional space on Sunday mornings has been met, and this part of the plan has been set aside for the moment. Whether it will become a necessity in the future is a question for those who follow to ponder.

Exportable/Transportable Products

The next part of our strategy plan is what we have chosen to call "exportable/transportable products." Our hope is to help other churches, especially those who are lacking in resources, live out their mission, as well as to help develop future leaders for our church. We state our goal in this way: To share The Garden's experience, knowledge, and resources with other churches, seminaries, and interested community organizations.

The way we have most often done that is by sharing our experiences at workshops and training events across the nation. We are also attempting to team with a university in our state to make some of our original video productions available for purchase by other interested parties. In addition, we are in the process of developing a database by theme and scriptural reference of all the music we have used over the last eight years; and eventually, we hope to make this database available for a nominal fee to other churches.

One approach currently being experimented with is a coaching process. Through The Garden's connection with Community Church of Joy in Phoenix, we have begun working with two other churches for a two-year period to help each of those congregations move toward the goals they have set for themselves. Through our individual contacts, as well as the times the three teams of leaders meet together, we are able to determine key issues and together suggest possible alternative ways to approach some of those issues. Although the success of this coaching process is yet to be seen, I really believe this is a viable way for us to assist others in achieving their goals. It can also be a time-consuming process that requires a fine balance of being available to help with other churches' needs, being able to deal with our own work, and caring for ourselves.

There's one more piece that fits into this part of our strategy plan, and that is the publication of written materials such as the book you have in your hand. The Worship Design Team recently completed a book of ten worship services we have offered around the theme of helping and serving. This book will serve to outline some of the work we have done and help the reader discover how some of our ideas might work in their setting. It remains to be seen if this will be the first or last such work.

Income Stream

An important issue for The Garden is also an element of our strategy plan, and that concerns an income stream for the continued vitality of our ministry. Our goal is to create a funding source or sources and income stream that are not totally dependent on attendees. Obviously, such a goal makes it possible for us to serve the population we feel we are called to serve. It also enables us to be creative and to reach more people. It takes away the necessity of pressuring attendees to support the ministry financially.

As one might imagine, this is a difficult issue for us. In a previous chapter, I spent some time discussing our philosophy of money and outlining the means for securing funds that we currently use. This is a topic that always seems to be part of our conversations both at Leadership Team and Development Team meetings. We realize fully that how we use our money has a lot to do with our faith and that giving is an important component of our faith journey. Because we understand that, we have chosen to take a more low-key approach to money in the worship service itself, and yet provide as much information and as many opportunities as possible to allow people to support The Garden financially.

We are fortunate to have the support of a congregation such as St. Luke's United Methodist Church behind us. Their willingness to support the clergy items of our budget is a tremendous advantage and alleviates the necessity of our underwriting that part of our ministry. Having space donated for our use is also a big plus for The Garden.

We continue to work intentionally toward identifying the sources of strongest support and nurturing those individuals and groups in a private way to increase their support, while at the same time raising the awareness of the congregation as a whole about the importance of supporting The Garden in every way possible—by prayers, attendance, time and talents, as well as by money. One additional way we are moving forward is through the establishment of an endowment (non-building) fund. We are in the early stages of such an undertaking, and it remains to be seen how that will continue. Hopefully, it will gain the kind of support we envision, and our future will be sound. Regardless of the financial circumstances in which we find ourselves, we continue to believe that God is good, that God's love is abundant, and that, if this ministry is meant to thrive, God will provide.

Creative Partnerships

Another section of our strategy plan is called Creative Partnerships, and it is simply the way we express our intention to form creative connections with other entities to enhance the work of The Garden. This term reflects the kind of relationship we have with Beef and Boards, the Mansion at Oak Hill, and St. Luke's; and it is the model we want to follow for finding other partners. It's important that all parties see the mutual benefit to be derived from integrating the church and the community, along with the higher visibility and expanded resources that are available to all partners. Sharing video and sound equipment, for example, is an advantage for both businesses with whom we work. The business partners provided the sound equipment, and we provided the video equipment at each site; and both The Garden and two businesses use sound and projection capabilities to their advantage.

I've mentioned other such partnerships that are under discussion. One is with the video production company with whom our video specialist works. We have teamed with the Indiana University School of Medicine and with the IU-Kenya AIDS project to provide funds for some of their medical resources. We are pursuing conversations about Internet potential with a university in our state. The possibilities are endless, and the advantages to all participants are unlimited. I really believe more churches should explore the options available in their communities; we might be surprised at what's out there.

Three- to Five-Year Staffing Plan

The last portion of our strategy plan is about staffing and says specifically that our goal is to provide training, succession, and long-term staff stability. The primary concern here is what will happen when the current leaders decide to retire or conclude that their work here is completed. In our United Methodist tradition, selection of the clergyperson for a church is the role of denominational officials. However, with a ministry as unique as The Garden, our Bishop and Cabinet have been very generous in allowing and encouraging us to search for those who feel they are called to this kind of ministry. We are always looking for viable candidates for the role of the spiritual leader of The Garden, as well as the other lead positions that are so vital to our well-being.

One of the ways we want to consider developing future leaders for The Garden and elsewhere is through the creation of an internship program. St. Luke's is really taking the lead in this endeavor and has a number of seminary students to whom a retired pastor is relating.

His goal is to help them discern their ministry, and to assist them in finding the support they need to develop into top-notch leaders.

We at The Garden have worked with a local seminary to provide a location for field education for qualified students. One of our key persons at Oak Hill came to The Garden through her seminary studies, and she has remained with us after her graduation and ordination. Another student is part of our Lead Team and is finding his mind expanded through the experience of working in a nontraditional setting. Both have been wonderful assets to our ministry, and they both have expanded our horizons as well.

A key position for us is that of our creative director. Suzanne Stark has been with The Garden since the very beginning, and her amazing talent will be very difficult to replace. We are hopeful of finding someone who is willing to work closely with her and to learn from her, and we are constantly looking for those who share our values, beliefs, and philosophy. I must add that the same is true for a number of our lead volunteers, who have added so much to the shape of The Garden, and who will be extremely hard to replace. Finding qualified, passionate, loving people is the key for us. People like those who currently commit themselves to The Garden are invaluable. Finding those who bring fresh perspectives is equally important.

I've outlined the principal parts of our strategy plan, and you might want to look over the original plan, which you will find in Appendix B of this book. Now I will be specific about where we are heading in the next two to three years. Being a part of Leadership Network's two-year multi-site community has caused us to be specific about what we hope to accomplish within the next two years. Our goals are these:

1. To add services at Oak Hill.
2. To add additional sites.
3. To create a strong Internet presence.
4. To create Garden-style children's programming.
5. To seek replacements for key leaders.
6. To get out of our box.

I will comment on a couple of these. Since we have backed away from buying or building a permanent space for The Garden, we have become intentional about being a multi-site ministry. We want to be both intentional about it and selective as to the sites we will consider. Thus, the first two goals reflect that direction as the main course for the future.

The last goal, that of getting out of our box, serves as a reminder to us that something new is always on the horizon, and we must be open to other ways of being The Garden. I doubt seriously that the future will see The Garden becoming more traditional. Instead, I think we will be searching for more creative, untried ways of being church. The challenge for a ministry is always success. Failure forces one to change and try something new, or at least it should force that move. With success, it's easy to become content with the way things are going and be unwilling to explore new avenues or try new ways of being. I hope and pray we never arrive at that point and, if we do, that God will give us a giant nudge and get us going again.

Questions for Consideration

1. What are the key issues that would be part of your church's strategy plan? How would you determine those issues, and what means do you have to address them?
2. What specific steps does your congregation need to take in the next two years to move forward?
3. What does tomorrow hold for you?

SEASON'S END

Everything that happens in this world happens at the time God chooses.   Ecclesiastes 3:1

In the fall, when days are becoming shorter and a chill is in the air, I usually go out to the flower beds that I planted in the spring and start pulling up the dead plants and discarding them. Many of us are familiar with the words that follow that initial verse in Ecclesiastes 3, and one of those verses advises us that there is indeed a time for planting and a time for pulling up.

There are many ways we could choose to interpret what the writer meant by this particular collection of beginnings and endings, but I'm choosing at this point to think that it says something to me about this book. It seems that the time was right to share the story of The Garden, and now it seems that the time is right to complete the writing. I want to thank Abingdon Press for giving me the opportunity to share a little bit about the ministry that has changed my life forever. This has been an adventure and a positive way for me to reflect on the past decade of my life and ministry and to sort out the critical elements that have made The Garden what it is.

Now it is time to hand the ball over to you, the readers. I hope and pray that God has spoken to you through these pages and that your ministry is better defined today than it was when you began reading. If this book has accomplished anything, I hope it has caused each reader to reflect on his or her own setting and to see new pos-sibilities. It is when we see the possibilities—the "new thing" that

Isaiah 43 talks about—that we can begin to step into a new future. Our church needs a new future; our past has been glorious, and I pray that our future be filled with the same glory. I know God will be guiding us into a new future; I pray that we have the courage to follow.

THE GARDEN'S ORIGINAL MINISTRY PLAN

St. Luke's Worship West at Beef and Boards Dinner Theatre

Goals

• To reach unchurched persons who have never been part of the church or inactive persons who have been disappointed by prior church experience.

• To use the meta model of ministry (small groups with well-trained, empowered leaders) as the underlying theology and structure.

• To create an environment that conveys the love of God for all persons and helps people experience the acceptance of a Christian community.

• To strengthen the outreach ministry of St. Luke's through this satellite off-site worship setting.

Objectives

- To present the proposal for this satellite worship to the Administrative Board on January 29, 1995.
- To introduce the idea to the congregation through the newsletter and pulpit announcements during February 1995.
- To begin the process of identifying and recruiting persons from the St. Luke's congregation to be a part of the start-up team for the new ministry.
- To begin intensive training for the small group leaders in March and continue for six months.
- To offer the first worship service at Beef and Boards no later than September 10, 1995, with at least two hundred people committed to attend and participate.
- To develop an alternative worshiping congregation composed of a core of persons from St. Luke's, their invited guests, and any others who respond to the marketing appeal.
- A tentative timetable for the development and implementation of this new off-site ministry is included at the end of the proposal.

Service—What Is Being Provided for This Gathering of People?

- A casual, informal, upbeat, joyful, relevant, inspiring time of gathering and worshiping.
- A theology/philosophy that is open, accepting, and seeking.
- A quality service that incorporates a variety of musical styles, some vignettes from stage and movies, fast-moving AV presentations, and brief and relevant messages.
- A setting that promotes informality, offering a bagel/fresh fruit/juice/coffee menu both before and during the service of worship.
- A service that consists of singing (often contemporary music or traditional music updated with a more contemporary sound), special

music, a time of prayer and reflection, a scriptural message of fifteen minutes in length, and a sending forth to share God's love.

- A message that relates to everyday life and how faith fits into our daily living.
- A service that is focused around relationship—with God and with others.
- A message that introduces the participants to the basic ideas of faith, such as God, Jesus, love, prayer, scripture, meaning and purpose in life, discovering who we are, joy, and laughter.
- A gathering that is oriented around the small group (meta) concept in which personal relationships and growth evolve.
- A gathering of people who will be able to participate in St. Luke's larger ministries, such as singles, youth, adult, or children's classes; grief or premarital support; and special services such as Maundy Thursday, Good Friday, and other high holy days when the theater would not be available.
- A service that has the capability of using modern technology and the resources that are available as a result of being housed in a theater.
- The doors to the theater would open at 8:30 A.M., and the service would likely begin at 9:00 A.M. It would last no more than forty-five minutes, and we would vacate the premises by 10:15 A.M. to accommodate the Beef and Boards operation schedule.
- Following the worship service, participants could gather in home groups for study and relationship building, or go to St. Luke's for children's classes, adult classes, or other special offerings at the 11:00 A.M. hour.
- While the service is casual and informal and "all-persons friendly," the need for childcare and some age-level gatherings is anticipated. Julia Skiles, St. Luke's Director of Children's Ministries, has agreed to assist with materials and ideas for fulfilling this need, and we would be able to find some appropriate space at the theater to have offerings for children concurrent with the worship service. Paid care for infants through three years old is included in the tentative budget.

Marketing: Who Is the Target and How Will They Be Reached?

- The target audience consists of the unchurched and inactive on the north side of Indianapolis and its environs. (No attempt is to be made at this point to become "site-specific.")
- The "start-up team" will consist of current St. Luke's members who have a pioneering spirit and are interested in beginning something new.
- This team will help shape the ministry to which they will want to invite at least one hundred who are unchurched or inactive.
- Others will be reached by the marketing campaign that will consist of both paid and free advertising, both "in-house" at St. Luke's and to the community.
- A marketing team (to be established) will design a campaign to promote the new ministry using whatever media is deemed most appropriate for the target group (radio, TV, cable, newspaper, direct mail, and so on).
- As much detailed information as possible will be gathered and stored regarding the individuals who respond to this ministry for follow-up and for better meeting their needs.

Organizational Approach

- Linda McCoy will be pastoral leader of this new ministry, spending one-half time with development of the new ministry and continuing ministry at St. Luke's. Other St. Luke's pastors might assist in this off-site ministry in the event of Linda's absence.
- The new satellite ministry will be organized around the team concept.
- These teams will be some of the ones created as this ministry idea becomes reality:
  - Start-up Team (those initiating the ministry)
  - Ministry Team (small group leaders designing how caring takes place)
  - Leadership Team (the core of persons heading the various areas of ministry)

- Worship Team (composed of pastor, music leader, technical expert, drama resource, and others as needed to shape each Sunday's worship experience)
- Technical Team (those who have expertise in lighting, sound, AV, video, graphic arts, and others)
- Education Team (those who are willing to help develop educational experiences for children and youth, if needed, on Sunday mornings, and for adults at other times of the week)
- Marketing Team (those responsible for designing and implementing the marketing plan to attract persons to the congregation)
- Development Team (those designated to develop additional sources of funding for the ministry)
- Outreach Team (those responsible for outlining areas of mission and ministry for the new gathering)
- Team leaders and members will be recruited from those who respond to the announcement of the ministry within St. Luke's and among those who are invited to be a part of this new ministry.
- Team leaders and members will participate initially in a team-building workshop.
- Team leaders will meet regularly for training, nurturance, and communication.
- Small group leaders (meta pastors) will meet weekly for four to six months for intensive training on leading small groups and empowering ministry.

Financing the New Ministry

- St. Luke's finance office will account separately all income and expenses of the new ministry.
- St. Luke's will support the new ministry by supplying the pastor's salary for this position, administrative space, and support staff as needed.
- Beef and Boards has agreed to donate the space for Sunday morning worship experience at the theater, located at 9301 N. Michigan Road, Indianapolis, Indiana.
- Additional funding for this new ministry is being sought from the South Indiana Conference Council on Ministries through the

subgroups New Church Development and Re-development, Urban and Suburban Ministries, and other areas such as experimental programs, new ministries, and any other avenues that might pertain to this creative ministry.

• It is anticipated that this ministry will be income/expense neutral. With additional funding along with the monies donated each Sunday, this off-site ministry will not be a drain on St. Luke's budget. Eventually, it is hoped that it will be a contributing factor to the budget and that it will open space for newcomers to take their place in the life of St. Luke's.

• Although it is difficult to ascertain that newcomers to the faith will be supportive financially, we expect new monies to be generated each Sunday.

• A preliminary yearly budget is attached to this proposal, along with a prorated 1995 budget that assumes a date no later than September 10, 1995, as the official start for the first worship experience for this new ministry and a March beginning for team-building and small group training.

Tentative Timetable

January 1995	Meet with Administrative Board for acceptance
February 1995	Announce and publicize idea to congregation
March 1995	Identify "pioneers" to serve as "start-up" team
March–August 1995	Team-building workshop an intensive training for small group pastors in the meta model
May–June 1995	Music leader and educational team begin Sunday-by-Sunday planning for worship
June 1995	First Worship service held at Beef and Boards (or when two hundred people in atten-

	dance is guaranteed, but no later than September 10, 1995)
September–December 1995	Implementation, evaluation, redesign of the ministry
January–December 1996	Increase worship attendance by at least one hundred people

THE GARDEN'S STRATEGY PLAN

Vision
The Garden is a celebration of life,
a journey into faith, and the soulful embrace of all.

Mission
The mission of The Garden is to engage all in the quest
to know and share the unconditional love of God.

Core Values

Spirituality	Inclusiveness
Love	Creative Excellence
Purposefulness	Empowerment
Celebration	

Fellowship and Education

Goal

• To create opportunities for spiritual, educational, and social connections among Garden children, youth, and adults.

Objectives

1. Develop and implement a development education series for all team leaders and staff **by Oct. 1, 2000**
2. Develop and enhance spiritual opportunities for constituents **by Oct. 1, 2000**
3. Develop and enhance social opportunities for constituents **by Oct. 1, 2000**
4. Develop Internet opportunities for interaction **by Jan. 1, 2001**

Action Steps

1. The Fellowship portion will be handled by The Bridge headed by Cindy Lively **Effective Now**
2. The second team will handle education opportunities (possibly called "The Path") **by Oct. 1, 2000**

Features

1. Small groups
2. Programs for integrating children, youth, and adults
3. Sports team
4. Special gatherings
5. Care teams
6. Food service
7. Gathering place
8. Web site
9. Task teams
10. Communication pieces
11. Retreat
12. Devotions
13. Prayer time

Benefits

- Greater feeling of connectedness
- Fun
- More visibility
- Knowledge building
- Support

• Sense of belonging
• Greater loyalty
• Disciples

Community Outreach

Goal

• To actively promote the spiritual and social health of the community.

Objectives

1. To expand the components of the charitable contributions giving program **by Oct. 1, 2000**
2. Develop opportunities for understanding of and appreciation for other faith paths and denominations **by Oct. 1, 2000**
3. Develop a spiritual growth Garden-sponsored event **by Oct. 1, 2000**

Action Steps

1. Solidify relation of The Garden with 10% Charitable Giving Organizations: i.e., video, Web link, flyers, and Communication Team **by Oct. 1, 2000**
2. Develop a plan to establish relationships and communications with other faith paths and denominations: i.e., guest speakers, educational seminars, and Web links **by Oct. 1, 2000**
3. Develop a plan to create alliances with social agencies for exchange of services: i.e., visiting nurses, blood bank, stress center **by Oct. 1, 2000**
4. Develop a plan to create a liaison with youth: i.e., Young Life, Fellowship of Christian Athletes, coffee house **by Oct. 1, 2000**

Features

1. Ten percent given to nonprofit grassroots groups in the metropolitan area

2. Sermons by other faiths (learning experience)
3. Expanded marketing efforts
4. Encouraging people to serve in community in ways that are meaningful to them
5. Videos for monthly charity to use in their fund-raising efforts
6. Nationally known speakers—lecture series
7. Identifying Garden outreach program
8. Video-conference in bar or some other facility

Benefits

• Increased community profile
• Reach more people
• Fulfills mission

Virtual Church

Goal

• To create a Virtual Garden.

Objectives

1. Create a "capacity" to further develop our Web page (audio, video, interactive, inspiration, education, and communication)
   by Nov. 1, 2000
2. Create a partnership with software/hardware companies
   by Jan. 1, 2001

Features

1. Weekly update
2. Mailing lists
3. Newsletters and lists
4. Resource reference library
5. Work group and special interest sections
6. Sound files—sermons and music

7. Moderated discussions
8. Interactive forums
9. Online study and development
10. Moderated discussion sessions
11. Streaming media capabilities, such as real-time broadcast of services
12. Web page links

Benefits

- Broader linkage to specific social service agencies
- Sharing God's love, and engage all in the quest
- Speaking to a population we would not reach otherwise
- Improved internal communication
- Learning
- Enhancing our ability to export services

Space*

Goal

- To create a multi-use facility that will contribute to the long-term operation and ministry of The Garden.

Values

- The Garden will not look like a traditional church inside or out.
- The Garden will have secular partners.
- The Garden location will be accessible to I-465 and preferably on the Northside.
- The Garden will have ample parking.
- The Garden will have additional space available for expansion.

* Please note that in 2004, The Garden's Leadership Team made a decision to be intentional and selective about becoming a multi-site ministry. This will eliminate the need for buying or building permanent space.

Space

- Identify The Garden's space needs   **Completed**
- Refine space needs   **by July 1, 2001**
  - Hire a professional (or seek a volunteer) to work with The Garden
  - Determine exact type and spaces needed now and in the future
  - Prioritize the need for each space
- Determine special equipment needs (for activities within the building sanctuary, media production, and so on) **by July 1, 2001**
- Hire an architect   **by July 1, 2001**
- Develop a cost estimate   **by Oct. 1, 2001**
- Secure financing   **by Jan. 1, 2002**
  - Hire a professional (or seek a volunteer) to work with The Garden
- Develop a budget   **by Mar. 1, 2002**
- Complete the design and blueprints process   **by June 1, 2002**
- Hire a Project Manager   **by July 1, 2002**
- Begin construction/remodeling   **by Aug. 1, 2002**

Location

- Identify preferable locations and possible sites   **by July 1, 2001**
  - Take a Garden census to determine a target area for new site
  - Identify available locations
  - Scout possible new locations
  - Make recommendations
- Finalize building and/or remodeling site location

                              by Jan. 1, 2002

  - Execute purchase/lease

Partners

- Coordinate efforts with Creative Partnership Team   **by Apr. 1, 2001**
  - Identify possible creative partners
  - Talk with interested individuals/groups
- Agree on partnership   **by July 1, 2001**
- Agree on type of facility and location   **by Sept. 1, 2001**

- Determine partner's space needs now and in the future
- Match The Garden's space needs with the partner's space
- Determine type of facility that fulfills space needs of The Garden and partner

Features

1. Public use and access
   theater
   conference center
   school/learning center
   retail space
   break-out rooms
2. Video projection
   live, on screen
3. Soundboard
4. Production capabilities
5. Video and audio recording
6. Tabletop "stuff"
7. Teleprompters
8. Team with partner
   production
   personnel
9. Food service/kitchen

Benefits

- Worship space for small group meetings, conference, children/youth, performing arts
- Provides income stream
- Rehearsal space
- Self-funding

Exportable/Transportable Products

Goal

- To share The Garden's experience, knowledge, and resources with other churches, seminaries, and interested community organizations.

Objectives

1. Develop a series of training events **by Jan. 2001**
2. Create a saleable package of Garden resources **by Mar. 2001**
3. Create the ability to share The Garden's worship experience on the Internet **by June 2001**
4. Develop the capacity to share The Garden's worship experience by satellite locations **by Jan. 2003**

Features

1. Workshops and training events that we host
2. Worship resources—music, video, whole service
3. Worship transmitted by Internet and TV
4. Satellite locations (franchise/video conference)
5. Performing arts
6. Internet—download sermons, music, audio Bible studies or classes, other courses
7. Audio
   - Sermon/service broadcast live
   - Garden radio via Internet
   - Discussion groups via Internet—live and moderated
   - Broadcast e-mail—inspirational, communication
   - Internal communications
   - Programs targeted to specific audiences
8. Video
   - Worship service
   - Lectures
   - Service on TV (traditional method and satellite)
   - Create multi-media CD-ROMs (visitors, membership, lectures, tour of church)

Benefits

- Helps other churches, especially those without resources
- Expands our visibility
- Helps develop future leaders
- Touches more lives
- Income stream
- Outlet for gifts and talents

- Target to specific audiences
- Fulfills creative excellence
- People more receptive because of anonymity
- Reaches around the world/on your timetable

Income Stream

Goal

- To create a funding source(s) and income stream not totally dependent on attendees.

Objectives

1. Establish an endowment for The Garden   **by Jan. 1, 2001**
2. Create the ability to fund 20 percent of The Garden's annual budget through grants   **by Jan. 1, 2001**
3. Create the ability to fund 50 percent of The Garden's annual budget through individual contributions   **by Jan. 1, 2001**
4. Create the ability to fund 30 percent of The Garden's annual budget through creative partnerships   **by Jan. 1, 2001**
5. Create a multi-use facility for The Garden that is income producing   **by Jan. 1, 2003**

Action Steps

1. Develop grant-writing program
   - Identify grant-writing team   **by Sept. 9, 2000**
   - Create program book   **by Nov. 1, 2000**
   - Identify grant prospects   **by Nov. 1, 2000**
2. Develop individual "Sunday offerings" program
   - Identify "Sunday offerings" team   **by Sept. 9, 2000**
   - Establish "Ways to Give" flyer   **by Nov. 1, 2000**
   - Printed financial information   **by Nov. 1, 2000**
3. Develop "Friends of the Garden" program
   - Identify "Friends of the Garden" team   **by Sept. 9, 2000**
   - Discern individuals with capacity to give   **by Dec. 1, 2000**

- Create opportunities to give/"Share Vision"   **by Dec. 1, 2000**
- Determine ways of thanking "Friends"   **by Dec. 1, 2000**
4. Develop "Creative Partnerships" program
  - Identify "Creative Partnerships" team   **by Sept. 9, 2000**
  - Identify potential partners   **by Jan. 1, 2001**
  - Determine ways to thank "Partner"   **by Jan. 1, 2001**

Features

1. Multi-use facility
2. Web site
3. Retail space
4. Endowment
5. Grants
6. Individual Contributions from a core group of attendees
7. Creative partnering
8. Philanthropic activity

Benefits

- Freedom to serve
- Freedom to be creative
- Reach more people
- Not reliant on pressuring attendees for financial support

Creative Partnerships

Goal

- To form creative partnerships to enhance The Garden's ministries.

Objectives

1. To work with St. Luke's on additional equipment
   by Jan. 1, 2001
2. To talk with developers about land acquisition and construction
   by Jan. 1, 2001
3. To create alliances with Social Agencies for exchange of services
   by Jan. 1, 2001

4. To be in conversation about youth coffee house
   by Jan. 1, 2001
5. To make contacts with other faiths and denominations
   by Oct. 10, 2000
6. To talk with businesses re: feasibility of joint facility use
   by Jan 1, 2001
7. To contact software/hardware companies re: Virtual Church
   by Jan. 1, 2001
8. To create liaisons with schools and seminaries
   by Jan. 1, 2001
9. To work with St. Luke's on production capabilities
   by Jan. 1, 2001
10. To work with film production companies re: licensing of film clips
    by Jan. 1, 2002

Action Steps

(See Action Steps for Income Stream, above.)

Features

1. Youth coffee house
2. St. Luke's—corporate sponsor
3. Developers
4. Multi-denominational organizations.
5. Charitable contribution organizations
   • POLIS Center
   • St. Vincent's
   • Technological companies
   • Schools
   • Seminaries
   • Hospitality industry
   • Film festival
6. Beef and Boards

Benefits

• Expanded resources
• Higher visibility
• Integration with community
• Increased community outreach
• Connections to new people
• Expanded programs

Three- to Five-Year Staffing Plan

Goal

• To provide training, succession, and long-term staff stability.

Objective

1. Leadership Team to develop and implement a plan of succession for all paid and nonpaid staff

Action Steps

1. To create internship through contacting seminaries and field placement agencies **by Oct. 1, 2001**
2. To create unpaid performing arts internship through contact with colleges and performing arts institutions **by Oct. 1, 2001**
3. Technical production—working with high school and college technical arts areas and with film producers. To find additional resource people. **by Oct. 1, 2001**
4. Create succession in the PowerPoint presentations. Contact J. Everett Light Center to recruit people with expertise in that area. **by Oct. 1, 2001**
5. To be continually recruiting people to give them experience and to help them share in the various aspects of paid and unpaid staffing **by Oct. 1, 2001**
6. To ensure succession in terms of key leadership, hospitality, communications, maketing and development **by Oct. 1, 2001**

Features

1. Ensured freshness of staff
2. Understood procedures for review of personnel
3. Ongoing assessment of quality and experience

Benefit

• Ensure continuity